WA

& HOWGILL FELLS

HILLSIDE GUIDES - ACROSS THE NORTH

- •JOURNEY OF THE AIRE   •JOURNEY OF THE WHARFE

Long Distance Walks
- •COAST TO COAST WALK   •DALES WAY   •CUMBRIA WAY
- •WESTMORLAND WAY   •FURNESS WAY   •NIDDERDALE WAY
- •BRONTE WAY   •CALDERDALE WAY   •PENDLE WAY

Circular Walks - Yorkshire Dales
- •East: NIDDERDALE & RIPON •West: THREE PEAKS & HOWGILL FELLS
- •WHARFEDALE   •MALHAMDALE   •WENSLEYDALE   •SWALEDALE

Circular Walks - Lancashire/North West
- •BOWLAND   •PENDLE & THE RIBBLE   •LUNESDALE
- •WEST PENNINE MOORS   •ARNSIDE & SILVERDALE

Circular Walks - North Pennines
- •EDEN VALLEY   •ALSTON & ALLENDALE

Circular Walks - Mid Yorkshire
- •HARROGATE & WHARFE VALLEY   •HOWARDIAN HILLS

Circular Walks - South Pennines
- •ILKLEY MOOR   •BRONTE COUNTRY   •CALDERDALE

Hillwalking - Lake District
- •LAKELAND FELLS - SOUTH   •LAKELAND FELLS - EAST
- •LAKELAND FELLS - NORTH   •LAKELAND FELLS - WEST

Short Scenic Walks
Yorkshire Dales
- •UPPER WHARFEDALE   •LOWER WHARFEDALE   •MALHAMDALE
- •UPPER WENSLEYDALE   •LOWER WENSLEYDALE   •SWALEDALE
- •NIDDERDALE   •SEDBERGH & DENTDALE
- •RIBBLESDALE   •INGLETON & WESTERN DALES
Northern England
- •HARROGATE & KNARESBOROUGH   •ILKLEY & WASHBURN VALLEY
- •AIRE VALLEY   •AMBLESIDE & LANGDALE   •AROUND PENDLE
- •RIBBLE VALLEY   •HAWORTH   •HEBDEN BRIDGE   •BOWLAND

Send for a detailed current catalogue and price list
and also visit www.hillsidepublications.co.uk

WALKING in YORKSHIRE

THREE PEAKS
& HOWGILL FELLS

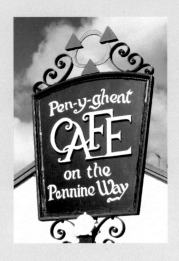

Paul Hannon

Hillside

HILLSIDE PUBLICATIONS

20 Wheathead Crescent
Keighley
West Yorkshire
BD22 6LX

First published in this format 2014
Previously published as *Three Peaks* (2009)
and *Howgill Fells* (revised 2014)

Cover illustrations: Crook of Lune Bridge; Penyghent
Back cover: Thornton Force; Page One: Stainforth Force
Page Three: Horton; Above: Dent; Opposite: The Spout, Carlingill
(Paul Hannon/Yorkshire Photo Library)

The sketch maps are based on 1947 Ordnance Survey One-Inch maps

Printed in China on behalf of Latitude Press

CONTENTS

INTRODUCTION

The western Yorkshire Dales is an area of very shapely hills intersected by beautiful valleys. The fells of Three Peaks country are of course dominated by the celebrated trio of Whernside, Ingleborough and Penyghent, while further north the Howgill Fells are a more compact, well-rounded group.

Three Peaks country features remarkable limestone formations and high mountains, with the famous triumvirate being very much the beacons that symbolize the area. As in the rest of the Dales, however, it is the valleys that really shape the countryside, and the two major dales are those of the Ribble and the Dee. Rising on the same moorland they immediately assume opposite directions, the Dee running north-west to Sedbergh and the Ribble south to Settle. They share a common disregard for Yorkshire, for while the Ribble is destined to become the major river of Lancashire, these days Dentdale is wholly Cumbrian. Lovely Dentdale happily remains enviably enshrouded in a near timeless quality, and forms a perfect cushion between the Three Peaks and the Howgills.

Whernside, Ingleborough and Penyghent are regular backdrops to most scenes in the district, and walkers come from afar to face their collective challenge. Within these pages can be found classic ascents of each of the Three Peaks, but hard going on the peaty heights is more often than not forsaken for the glories of limestone country. Along the flanks of these great mountains is an array of gleaming scars and pavements, an unparalleled assembly of gaping potholes and labyrinthine caves, sparkling waterfalls and a network of inviting green trackways over the hills. Settle is a buzzing little town that makes a perfect base for the south of the area, and is supported by a delectable range of villages such as Stainforth and Langcliffe, Horton and Austwick, Clapham and Ingleton.

The Howgill Fells occupy the north-western corner of the Yorkshire Dales: triangular in shape, the group is moated by the River Lune on two sides and the Rawthey on the other. The terrain of the Howgills is such that it encourages long strides over its grassy ridges, a lack of internal walls instilling a sense of freedom not sensed elsewhere in the Dales. Rarely in evidence is the underlying slate, though when revealed it is done in spectacular style, at the quite remarkable ravines of Cautley and Carlin Gill. This walkers'

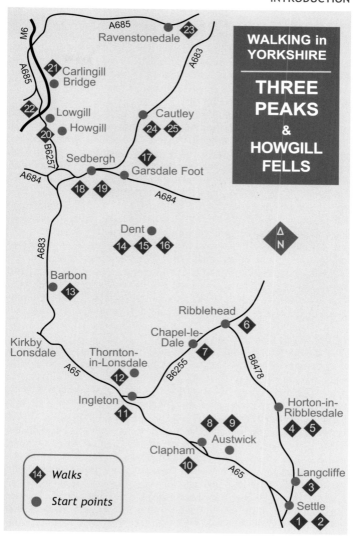

paradise is a no-man's-land where Dales and Lakes meet, with the characteristics of both present without either dominating. The hub of this otherwise sparsely populated district is Sedbergh, largest community in the National Park, which sits regally at the foot of its fells and presides over the convergence of several rivers.

The Settle-Carlisle Railway

The Settle-Carlisle Railway runs the length of Ribblesdale and encircles the heads of Dentdale and Garsdale, a monument to Victorian enterprise that is as much a part of the district as the very hills. It was completed in 1876, after seven hard years of work as the Midland Railway created their own main line to Scotland. With more sensible routes to east and west, they resorted to the challenge of the high Pennines. Logical approaches via Ribblesdale and the Eden Valley led to the central massif from Ribblehead to Mallerstang, and this gave rise to the spectacular feats of engineering you see today, as deep tunnels alternate with tall viaducts.

During construction work, thousand of 'navvies' filled extensive shanty towns: with an air of the Wild West these were lively places, and with little else on which to spend money, well-frequented and equally temporary inns witnessed regular outbreaks of violence. Through illnesses like smallpox and construction accidents, churchyards at Cowgill and Chapel-le-Dale were literally overflowing.

Access to the countryside

The majority of walks are on public rights of way with no access restrictions, or long-established access areas and paths. A handful also take advantage of the 2004 implementation of Right to Roam: any walks making use of Open Country are noted as such in their introduction, though on most days of the year you are free to walk responsibly over these wonderfully invigorating landscapes. Of the restrictions that do pertain, the two most notable are that dogs are normally banned from grouse moors (other than on rights of way); and that the areas can be closed to walkers for up to 28 days each year, subject to advance notice. The most likely times will be from the 'Glorious Twelfth', the start of the grouse shooting season in August, though weekends should largely be unaffected. Further information can be obtained from the Countryside Agency, and ideally from information centres. Finally, bear in mind that in spring, avoiding tramping over open country away from paths would help safeguard the crucial period for vulnerable ground-nesting birds.

Though bus services within the area are generally limited, availability, if any, is mentioned in the introduction to each walk. There are railway stations at Giggleswick, Clapham, Settle, Horton, Ribblehead, Dent Head, Garsdale Head and Kirkby Stephen.

Using the guide

The walks range from 4 to 7½ miles, with the average distance being just under 6 miles. Each walk is self-contained, with essential information followed by a concise route description and a simple map. Dovetailed in between are snippets of information on features along the way: these are in *italics* to ensure that the all important route details are easier to locate. Start point postcodes are a rough guide only for those with 'satnav': grid references are more precise!

The sketch maps serve to identify the location of the routes rather than the fine detail, and whilst the description should be sufficient to guide you around, the appropriate Ordnance Survey map is recommended. To gain the most from a walk, the detail of a 1:25,000 scale Explorer map is unsurpassed. It also gives the option to vary walks as desired, giving a much improved picture of your surroundings and the availability of any linking paths for shortening or lengthening walks. Three maps cover all the walks:

• *Explorer OL2 - Yorkshire Dales South/West (covers 15 walks)*
• *Explorer OL19 - Howgill Fells/Upper Eden Valley*
• *Explorer OL41 - Forest of Bowland & Ribblesdale (needed for 1)*
Also very useful for planning is Landranger map 98, with small parts also featuring on sheets 91 and 97.

Useful contacts
Yorkshire Dales National Park
• 01756-751600   www.yorkshiredales.org.uk
Information Centres
Town Hall **Settle** • 01729-825192
Community Centre **Ingleton** • 015242-41049
Penyghent Cafe **Horton-in-Ribblesdale** • 01729-860333
72 Main Street **Sedbergh** • 015396-20125
24 Main Street **Kirkby Lonsdale** • 015242-71437
Market Square **Kirkby Stephen** • 017683-71199
Open Access • 0845-100 3298   www.countrysideaccess.gov.uk

VICTORIA CAVE

Classic, gleaming limestone country overlooking Settle

START *Settle (SD 819636; BD24 9EJ)*

DISTANCE *5³4 miles (9km)*

ORDNANCE SURVEY 1:25,000 MAP
Explorer OL2 - Yorkshire Dales South/West **or**
Explorer OL41 - Forest of Bowland & Ribblesdale

ACCESS *Start from the town centre. Car parks. Bus from Skipton and Ingleton. Station on the Settle-Carlisle line.*

Settle is a bustling little town that is an important focal point for an extensive rural area. It is invariably busy, being a long established halting place for those bound further afield, and also ideally centred for the Three Peaks district. Market day (Tuesday) presents the liveliest scene, when the small square is awash with colour. The town boasts numerous old buildings, some hidden and others very much on display. Facing the square is the historic row known as the Shambles, with its shops peeping from behind archways: the lower section dates back to the 17th century. Nearby is the Folly, a large, rambling 17th century house with an intricate façade. As home to the Museum of North Craven Life it gives a rewarding insight into the district's past, while the limestone cliff of Castleberg provides a dramatic bird's-eye view of the town today. Also facing the square is a former inn 'the Naked Man', its *appropriate carved sign being dated 1633 and a source of some humour. Settle was by-passed by the A65 in 1988. The parish church of the Holy Ascension stands at the northern end of town and dates from 1838. Also of note are the Town Hall (1833), Victoria Hall (1853), and the Friends' Meeting House (1689).*

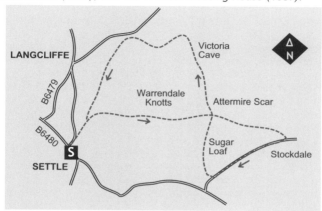

Leave the market place by Constitution Hill to the left of the Shambles. After a steep pull the road turns left, and almost at once abandon it in favour of the rougher Banks Lane, to the right. This resumes the climb between walls to emerge into open country. *Already there are big views back over Settle and Giggleswick to the Bowland moors, while Ingleborough appears before the lane ends.* At once the way forks: take the right branch slanting up the bank, passing through an old wall and then quickly turning to ascend more directly. Merging with a wall from the left it rises to a gate at the top. Keep on, the early fork giving alternative options on broad grassy paths that will shortly merge. Now level, ahead is the magnificent scenery of Warrendale Knotts and Attermire Scar. The path drops down into this upland bowl, over a stile and along to a gateway below Attermire Scar. *Attermire Cave is a dark slit high up the cliff. For those agile enough to reach its entrance, it can be penetrated a fair way with a sense of adventure and a reliable torch. Just prior to the gateway are the remnants of a shooting range.* The route returns you here after a loop around Sugar Loaf.

To enjoy the loop bear right through the gateway, a good path running a level course beneath the receding scar, and soon rising through several pastures - bridle-gates all the way - to merge with a wall leading along to a gate onto Stockdale Lane. *Views across this secluded side valley are dominated by Rye Loaf Hill's rounded dome.* Turn right on the lane for a gentle descent. *This gives ample time to further appraise Warrendale Knotts: further afield are the Lancashire heights of Pendle Hill, Waddington Fell and the edge of Bowland.* After a slight rise to a brow the road drops to a sharp bend left. Here leave by a gate/stile and take the track ascending right with a wall. *On the modest brow stands an old limekiln, while the Warrendale Knotts scene returns ahead.* A broad grassy path runs on through undulating pasture, passing beneath the mini peak of Sugar Loaf Hill and along to a gate in a fence. It then drops gently towards a gate ahead to rejoin the earlier route, though properly you fork right on a gentler path to a wall-stile to its right.

Back at the gateway, pass through again and take the wallside path rising to a nick, then on through a trough on a fine green way. *Ingleborough and Whernside fill the open view ahead.* A wall joins you to rise to a kissing-gate ahead, and a thinner path resumes alongside the wall beneath scree at the foot of a limestone scar. The entrance to Victoria Cave can be gleaned by the wall of clean rock above it, and a thin path detours up to it. Before approaching it, consider the dire warnings of the perils of rockfalls. *The massive entrance has been blasted to this size in modern times, but the cave's history goes back through countless periods. It has yielded evidence of richly varied occupancy, including bones of rhinoceros, hippopotamus, bear, mammoth and Stone Age man.* Another path slants back down to the main one to resume, quickly reaching a kissing-gate onto the unsurfaced Gorbeck Road.

Turn left through the gate and descend the track to the road climbing out of Langcliffe. At once, however, take a bridle-gate on the left and a splendid path heads away, passing beneath a wood and above a steep fall to Langcliffe. *Behind you is a fine prospect of Penyghent.* Two more bridle-gates are met before the path curves down a big sloping pasture to a bridle-gate at the end. Through this follow a wall away, merging with a lower bridleway a little further. Remain on this, being briefly enclosed, then on to merge with the outward route to descend Banks Lane back into town.

STAINFORTH FORCE

A rare stretch of Ribble-side walking to a memorable scene

START *Settle (SD 819636; BD24 9EJ)*

DISTANCE *5³⁄4 miles (9km)*

ORDNANCE SURVEY 1:25,000 MAP
Explorer OL2 - Yorkshire Dales South/West **or**
Explorer OL41 - Forest of Bowland & Ribblesdale

ACCESS *Start from the town centre. Car parks. Bus from Skipton and Ingleton. Station on the Settle-Carlisle line.*

For a note on Settle see page 10. From the Town Hall by the market square cross the main road and head down Kirkgate. En route you pass Victoria Hall and the Friends' Meeting House. Under the railway bridge keep straight on, passing an attractive Georgian house on the right and a supermarket on the left. At the bend leave the road and go on a footway left of the fire station. At the end swing right to pass round the back of Kings Mill, a recent conversion to residential use. Go left to cross a footbridge over the Ribble and turn upstream on the urban footway to the main road bridge.

Cross the road and head straight off along an enclosed path between sports fields. *Ahead, Penyghent looks magnificent.* At the end join the river briefly before being ushered away into a field. Cross to a prominent stile at the far end to enjoy a good section above a steep wooded riverbank: directly below is Langcliffe paper

13

mill. Emerging again, this time bear left to a stile onto Stackhouse Lane. Turn right to reach the edge of Stackhouse. *This cosy little grouping of exclusive dwellings huddles beneath the hill and is clearly happy to remain hidden in its protective greenery.* A short loop gives a slightly closer look: take the first rough road into it, turning first right along what becomes a grassy cart track, then right again back onto the road. Just a few yards further, take a walled green path to the right to meet the Ribble at the Locks, an attractive scene that incorporates a weir.

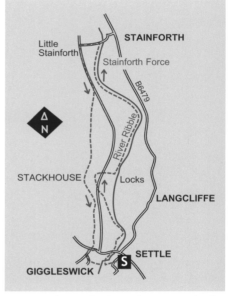

Using the footbridge only as a viewpoint, instead turn upstream with the river. At the end of a long pasture after an old paper mill you are briefly parted from the Ribble, passing a lively spring, but that aside, its bank leads unerringly to Stainforth Bridge. Just beyond the entry of Stainforth Beck you reach the delightful waterplay of Stainforth Force. *The combination of bridge, riverbank, waterfall and adjacent caravan site make this a place of very popular resort. The idyllically sited falls are a rare burst of activity for the Ribble.* Just beyond the falls you join a narrow back road alongside Stainforth Bridge. *This graceful 17th century structure was built to serve the York-Lancaster packhorse trade.* Without crossing it turn left to ascend the little road up past the caravan site to a junction at Little Stainforth. *Also known as Knight Stainforth, this tiny hamlet is dominated by the three-storey hall dating largely from the 17th century.*

Turn left along Stainforth Lane for a few minutes to reach a stile on the right, in a dip. *Immediately before it stands an old Giggleswick-Stainforth boundary stone on the verge, while the smashing view features the River Ribble, Stainforth village and Fountains Fell.* Head directly away, contouring across the field aiming between two barns further ahead. A stile will be located as you approach the wall, the first of a string that maintain a near straight line through the fields. *Looking back, mighty Penyghent rises impressively over the valley.* Only on approaching a wood do you deflect right outside it, on through a gateway where a cart track leads down to a path junction at the rear of the hamlet of Stackhouse. Go straight on beneath trees outside the wall, the track running to a gate onto Stackhouse Lane, where you walked earlier.

Don't join the road, however, but advance straight on the field bottom. The way runs on via another stile with the road just below, and after crossing a drive to a stile, contour straight across the field to a stile by the bottom of Lord's Wood. *Settle is in view just ahead.* Ignoring a stile into the trees turn left on an embanked path that runs along a field top to a gap-stile towards the end, beyond the wood. Cross over the cart track and head away along a broad, enclosed path, rising gently to soon reach the end of a suburban street, The Mains. This drops down onto the main road through Giggleswick, opposite the Harts Head pub.

Cross and turn right down Belle Hill, and while your route is left along Bankwell Road, first venture briefly right on Church Street. *Giggleswick is a real labyrinth of delights, countless cottages with centuries-old datestones huddling near the ancient church of St Alkelda. This archetypal English scene also includes the hugely characterful Black Horse pub, also of some age: outside stands the old market cross, while across the street is the village shop. The railway station is virtually a mile distant across the by-pass. Founded in 1507 the highly regarded public school is best known to passers-by for the dome of its chapel, conspicuous in many views in the district.* Just round a bend on Bankwell Road take a snicket hidden between tall walls on the left: this path runs on to emerge back onto the riverbank by the footbridge at the start of the walk. Re-cross the bridge and retrace your opening steps back into the centre of Settle.

CATRIGG FORCE

*A magnificent waterfall in a wooded ravine is well
supported by big views and a fascinating industrial relic*

START *Langcliffe (SD 822650; BD24 9LY)*

DISTANCE *4³4 miles (7¹2km)*

ORDNANCE SURVEY 1:25,000 MAP
Explorer OL2 - Yorkshire Dales South/West **or**
Explorer OL41 - Forest of Bowland & Ribblesdale

ACCESS *Start from the village centre. Car park. Settle-Horton bus.*

Langcliffe is a lovely village with many attractive buildings
and a spacious green. Of particular interest is the hall, dating
from the 17th century. By the phone box look for a tablet on a
house wall depicting the Naked Woman, and modestly dated 1660.
Once an inn, it was probably a close friend of Settle's more famous
Naked Man. Leave the car park on a walled rough lane at the left
side. Quickly reaching a junction, turn right to commence a lengthy
stride on what rapidly becomes a gem of a green lane all the way
to its demise. *Ahead is the edge of the quarried Stainforth Scar.*
Opt for the right-hand gate to run along the field-top, and from the
gate at the far end a path climbs steeply above the lip of the old
quarry. *Look back over fields decorated with the strip lynchets of
early farmers, with the hamlet of Stackhouse and a good section
of river on view.*

A small gate in the top corner is the key to continuing up the next smaller enclosure, which is left by a gate/stile to the right of a walled green way heading left. Rise up a field centre to a stile onto Lower Winskill's drive, turning right to the entrance to Upper Winskill Farm. Turn right on the access road which rises steadily past Winskill Stones to join the Malham Moor road. *On a clear day pause here to appraise Lakeland's distant Coniston Fells.* Turn left along this unfenced strip of tarmac between limestone outcrops. *An old limekiln sits on the right before the brow, which then reveals a fine skyline featuring the heights of Penyghent, Plover Hill and Fountains Fell.*

Just before dropping down towards a cattle-grid, double back left down an inviting-looking cart track. This now slants down through several enclosures with Ingleborough dominant ahead. Remain on this all the way down to the bottom corner of a field with a prominent clump of trees behind: this marks

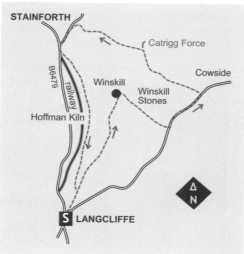

the location of Catrigg Force. Through the gate is the head of Goat Scar Lane. Before heading down it, first savour the waterfall detour. Through a small gate on the right a short path drops down to the top of the waterfall, where with great care you can peer down to the bottom. The conventional view can be sampled by entering the trees on the left to descend a good path to the foot of the ravine. *This is as lovely as any waterfall in the Dales.* Returning to Goat Scar Lane turn down its stony, enclosed course all the way into Stainforth, emerging onto a green.

Stainforth is a sizeable village stood high above and back from the Ribble, and long since by-passed by the road up the dale. Centrally located is the Craven Heifer, a pleasant, multi-roomed pub sporting a popular local name, and that for an enterprising spell doubled as a Post office. St Peter's church dates from 1842. A particularly pleasing corner can be found where stepping-stones cross the beck by a small green. Stainforth's best known features, its packhorse bridge and waterfall on the Ribble, are to be found outside the village (see WALK 2). Also on the village edge is the imposing mansion of Taitlands, a youth hostel for around 60 years until closure in 2007.

Go left from the pub south along the street to join the valley road. Just a short way along the footway take a stile on the left and head along the field to a gate/stile. *Stainforth Scar is cloaked in trees up to the left.* Continue on towards the end of the next field where a fence-stile puts you into the environs of the former

Craven Lime Works. An informative trail has been devised, and a short choice awaits here. Either go left for the old winding house and then down an incline, or right for the massive triple draw kilns of 1872. The paths rejoin beyond them to run to a wall-stile across a slab bridge, now revealing the amazing Hoffman Kiln in front.

This is the piece de resistance of the site, the most impressive limekiln in the country. On your left is a tunnel entrance through which horse-drawn waggons brought blocks of limestone out of the quarry above:

constructed in 1873, the kiln features 22 individual chambers, and working round the clock it occupied no less than 90 workers at its peak. At the far end drop down into a car park. Pass to the left of the house and follow the access road out, passing another car park and a red-brick weigh house. *Just after this a short path detours back left up to the remains of the Spencer Kilns, which produced a purer form of lime.* Just further the road swings right to pass under the railway to join the valley road.

Don't pass under the bridge, however, but take an enclosed cart track on the left on the near side of the line. *Below you is the Ribble.* Through a gate/stile at the end the track emerges into a field. Undulating pleasantly along towards the far side, as it turns uphill you keep straight on to a stile just ahead. A thinner path takes up the running, crossing to a stile on a gentle brow. *Look back here to appraise a fine prospect up the valley.* Continue to a stile ahead, then bear left across to a corner stile onto the grassy lane on which you began. Turn right on this the short way back into Langcliffe.

Catrigg Force

Opposite:
At the
Hoffman Kiln

Moughton Scars

*A simple excursion around the limestone scars of Sulber
and Thieves Moss, with superb views across to Penyghent*

START *Horton-in-Ribblesdale (SD 808726; BD24 0HF)*

DISTANCE *5$\frac{1}{2}$ miles (9km)*

ORDNANCE SURVEY 1:25,000 MAP
Explorer OL2 - Yorkshire Dales South/West

ACCESS *Start from the village centre. National Park car park.
Bus from Settle. Station on the Settle-Carlisle line.*
•OPEN ACCESS - see page 8.

Horton-in-Ribblesdale is the first village in a valley which
ends in the Irish Sea beyond Preston, and is very much the centre
of Three Peaks country. It has little intrinsic charm, being an odd
mixture of dwellings strung along the road, and overlooked by a
large quarry. Several cottage datestones go back to the late 17th
century. Horton's real attraction is its location, as the sight of
countless boots being pulled on in its car park testifies: there is a
true walkers' atmosphere here. There is a popular campsite and a
renowned cafe that caters for the weary, while pubs are found at
either end. The Crown has two arched bridges outside, while the
Golden Lion faces St Oswald's church with its Norman doorway.

From the Penyghent Cafe head north into the car park and cross the footbridge at its northern end to by-pass the road bridges by the Crown Hotel. Over the Ribble remain on the roadside footway to a junction at the end. Go straight ahead up a driveway towards the station, taking a small gate to the left onto the platform. Cross the line with care and a little path rises into a field. The path crosses to a small gate just ahead, with the farm at Beecroft Hall appearing. Bear right, the path crossing a large field to the farm drive, with a stile in the wall beyond. It crosses another large field, swinging left further on and up to a gate into a sloping limestone pasture. The path slants up and left across this to run to a gateway in an old wall. It heads away to fork just 150 paces further. The route in front is your return, but for now take the Austwick fork which bears left as a broad green way, ignoring an early branch doubling back up to the right. With Moughton ahead, it crosses to a gate at the wall corner to the right. *Before reaching the gate, Ingleborough slides majestically into your view.*

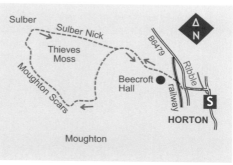

The splendid path continues along the wallside ahead, with heather to either side. Towards the end it crosses a stile in the wall, and heads directly away with a line of old stone grouse butts. After several of these the path swings left through them and bears off to rapidly reach a major turning point as you look down on the green floor of Crummack Dale. While the Austwick path descends here, your route is the thin path doubling back up to a prominent cairn to the right, just above. The little path now begins a classic traverse around the rim of Moughton Scars, above a substantial limestone escarpment with Thieves Moss to the right. *The Bowland skyline rises beyond the Wenning Valley, shortly to be joined by Pendle Hill.* A wall quickly comes up for company but after a while drops away again. Remain on the edge, largely with a thin path as

21

you curve round, partly on a limestone pavement, to reach another wall just below, where the Beggar's Stile crosses it.

Drop down onto and bear right along the inviting green path, which quickly slants more onto the plateau and crosses limestone pavements towards the other side. At the end of the limestone it merges with a path from the right, bearing left on it for a short pull up a minor scree slope to the rim above, a good place to linger. Pass through the small gate just ahead to join a grassy bridleway. Turn right through the gate/stile and head away on it, just a few minutes' walk to the path crossroads at Sulber. Here the path ascending Ingleborough from Horton crosses the Austwick-Selside bridleway. Rejoining the Ingleborough path, turn right on its course through the distinct trough of Sulber Nick. *The wayward staggering of Three Peakers is evident in the state of the path after a wet spell. Looking back, Ingleborough quickly returns to view.* At the end of the nick it drops down to a bridle-gate in a wall and runs on to rejoin the outward route. All that remains is to retrace steps back to Horton, fully savouring the awesome picture of Penyghent straight ahead.

On Moughton Scars, looking to Ingleborough

PENYGHENT

The classic ascent route of the easiest of the Three Peaks: its popularity doesn't stop this being a grand excursion

START *Horton-in-Ribblesdale (SD 808726; BD24 0HF)*

DISTANCE *5^{1}2 miles (9km)*

ORDNANCE SURVEY 1:25,000 MAP
Explorer OL2 - Yorkshire Dales South/West

ACCESS *Start from the village centre. National Park car park. Bus from Settle. Station on the Settle-Carlisle line.*

For a note on Horton see page 20. From the Penyghent Cafe head south along the road, turning off left along a short-lived field path just prior to the churchyard. It emerges onto a back road, which is followed left, and the beck is crossed almost at once by a footbridge. Go left on the lane opposite, past the school and up the winding lane to approach Brackenbottom. *En route, over to the left is the prominent Douk Gill Head, the resurgence of the waters entering the mighty chasm of Hull Pot, which will be visited on the descent. The farming hamlet of Brackenbottom spreads around a small green and features several roadside stone troughs. It also incorporates a caving club's base.*

At the start of the hamlet a gate on the left sends a pleasant path heading up the side of a field. *Wide views back over the village see Ingleborough rising above the Horton quarry.* On approaching

23

a stile the magnificent profile of your mountain reveals itself, an inspirational objective. The clear route of ascent is entirely uncomplicated as the path continues up in style through modest bands of limestone, continuing above these to eventually, after one or two ups and downs, gain a stile at the foot of Penyghent's south ridge proper, and earn views eastwards to Fountains Fell.

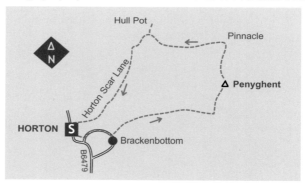

Over the stile, turn left up the wallside for the final push, which comprises two distinct halves. First you tackle the limestone band, then after a respite, clamber up through a boulderfield to engage the upper, gritstone band. Beyond this you are virtually on the top, and a simple stroll leads up to the OS column, cairn and modern shelter. *At 2277ft/694m Penyghent's summit is a grand place to be, with extensive views over Three Peaks country and beyond. Dales heights on view include, clockwise, Ingleborough, Simon Fell, Whernside, the Howgill Fells, Baugh Fell, Widdale Fell, Dodd Fell, Great Shunner Fell, Plover Hill, Yockenthwaite Moor, Penhill, Buckden Pike, Great Whernside, Darnbrook Fell, Fountains Fell, Grizedales and Rye Loaf Hill: Pendle Hill and the Bowland moors fill a large area to the south.*

Leave by crossing the stile and heading along the broad path slanting away. This quickly reaches a well-defined edge above gritstone outcrops, and thence deflects northwards to work down to the limestone band. *Penyghent's gritstone buttresses are the only place on the Three Peaks to attract the attention of rock climbers.* A path junction is a major turning point, as you begin the infallible direct descent on one of the earliest sections of rebuilt paths on the Three Peaks. First, however, a look along to the right will reveal the spectacular finger of rock known as Penyghent Pinnacle. *This limestone spire is only evident at close quarters, otherwise its detachment from the line of crags is not seen.*

Your path, meanwhile, works straight down the fell, with the gaping hole of Hull Pot unmistakable down on the moor below. The path descends through a couple of gates and along to the head of Horton Scar Lane. Shortly before the second gate, the sinister slit of Hunt Pot can be located to the left just off the path. *Caution is urged if peering in, for its depth is something like 200 feet.* Before turning down the lane, go right for five level minutes along a broad, grassy track to arrive at Hull Pot. *This magnificent chasm in the heart of the moors is a remarkable contrast to Hunt Pot. Roughly 300 feet long and 60 feet wide, it is seen at its best when a waterfall plunges over the northern edge: under normal conditions this will have sunk underground before reaching the hole.* Back at the lanehead simply follow the rough, walled track all the way down to the village, enjoying views across to Penyghent's familiar profile and over the valley. You emerge, fittingly, opposite the Penyghent Cafe.

Fountains Fell from Penyghent

WHERNSIDE

A reasonably demanding walk to the highest point in the Yorkshire Dales: firm paths virtually throughout

START Ribblehead (SD 764792; LA6 3AS)

DISTANCE $7^1{}_2$ miles (12km)

ORDNANCE SURVEY 1:25,000 MAP
Explorer OL2 - Yorkshire Dales South/West

ACCESS Start from the road junction below the pub. Ample parking between junction and pub. Station on the Settle-Carlisle line, seasonal Sunday bus from Ingleton.

The highest of Yorkshire's Three Peaks is the least popular, and though Whernside cannot fashion the shapely profile of its two colleagues, it nevertheless provides a grand walk. The various forms of pathwork encountered offer an insight into the path construction over the years of the Three Peaks Project. Ribblehead stands at the junction of two important Dales roads, where that from Settle meets the Ingleton-Hawes road. Only buildings are the Station Inn and some old railway cottages. The pub features a bunkhouse and one of the finest gents' toilet views in the land. It is of course the railway that earned national fame for Ribblehead, in the shape of its 24-arch viaduct. More properly Batty Moss Viaduct, this symbol of Victorian enterprise also became the symbol of a successful campaign to prevent closure of the line in the 1980s.

From the road junction a path runs along to meet the broad track heading for the viaduct. Just before its arches, branch right on a clear path which runs parallel to the railway line. *Already, as for most of the walk, all Three Peaks are well displayed.* After a brief pull simply remain on the path shadowing the railway. It runs by the romantically sited Blea Moor signal box before straying a little from the line, crossing one arm of a beck and following the other to the last bridge (an aqueduct) before Blea Moor Tunnel. *By far the longest tunnel on the Settle-Carlisle Line, it was built in the 1870s and burrows under the moor for some 2630ft/800m. The central, deepest shaft is more than 350ft/106m above the line.*

Across the aqueduct keep to the reconstructed path which rises to a stile in the fence ahead. This yields a splendid view of Force Gill, with the lower of its two fine waterfalls well portrayed.

From the stile the path rises left, climbing steepishly alongside the fence. The summit ridge returns to view, and at a step-stile in the adjacent fence, cross and resume on the main path. *The ascending, much less-trafficked path continues over the shoulder of the fell and into Dentdale, a former packhorse route known as the Craven Way.*

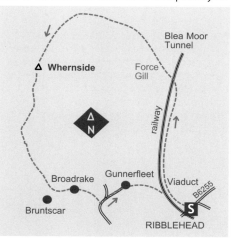

Now feeling to be on the fell proper, the excellently restored path climbs more steadily to meet a fence and old wall, thence slanting left with them to gain the northern end of Whernside's summit ridge by way of a long series of old flagstones. *From this corner look behind to see Artengill Viaduct well displayed and dwarfed, directly beneath Widdale Fell. Through the gap to the left are Mallerstang Edge and Wild Boar Fell (just).* The finest section ensues as the path runs along the crest of the increasingly steep eastern plunge. *Looking back, the Howgill Fells take their place in an expanding view, with the green floor of Dentdale appearing: a clear day brings the Lakeland Fells into place far beyond. Contrastingly close, just beneath your scarp is Greensett Tarn, while Whernside Tarns are seen on the plateau to the north.*

Though there is still a bit of work needed to gain the summit, it is nevertheless soon reached in this pleasant situation. An Ordnance Survey column at 2415ft/736m stands through a stile in a kink of the wall, adorned with a modern shelter. *Whernside's views are of a sweeping Dales landscape to the east, mile upon mile of brown rolling fells. Across to the west the Gragareth-Great Coum ridge is seen in its entirety. Penyghent is well seen too, but it is mighty Ingleborough that earns the accolades across the limestone scars of Chapel-le-Dale. In the other direction, Dentdale leads the eye to the Howgill Fells, while further west a clear day reveals an extensive distant prospect of the Lakeland Fells.*

Resume on the wallside path, for some time before making two short, stony descents. Your path then leaves the broadening ridge, dropping left to make a rapid descent to the valley. *A contrastingly grand little path remains on the ridge, bound for distant Ingleton. Ingleborough, meanwhile, increasingly dominates the descent.* The first section is not too rapid, however, as the upright stones of the built path defy anyone to move at anything above a cautious pace.

Beneath a wall-stile easier progress is made, and a stile into a final pasture sees limestone terrain ease the way down to meet a short-lived lanehead in the corner beyond limestone outcrops. Go right a few paces to a T-junction of ways alongside an old limekiln, but just before it, take a bridle-gate on the left and cross the field to Broadrake. *Note the line of farmsteads set under the base of the long limestone terrace, taking advantage of the presence of a spring-line.*

At Broadrake Farm, turn right down the drive. As it goes right and crosses a cattle-grid, bear left on a grassy track over rough pasture. At an early fork go left to a gate/stile. The green track then heads away to ford normally dry Winterscales Beck. If not dry, turn briefly downstream to where it should sink below ground at Gatekirk Sinks. Across, it curves less clearly right to join a surfaced road. *Enclosed in trees on the right is the impressive ravine of Gatekirk Cave.* Turn left on this farm drive until a fork just after it has bridged the beck: go right through a couple of fields to Gunnerfleet Farm. Take the bridge on the right (the lively beck is on the surface here!) and pass along the nearside of the buildings and away along a firm track. This leads back under the viaduct to finish. *Beneath the viaduct a monument celebrates its restoration.*

Opposite: Ingleborough from Whernside   Whernside from Bruntscar

INGLEBOROUGH

A steep but easy ascent of the Dales' landmark mountain

START *Chapel-le-Dale (SD 742776; LA6 3AR)*

DISTANCE *5^{1}4 miles (8^{1}2km)*

ORDNANCE SURVEY 1:25,000 MAP
Explorer OL2 - Yorkshire Dales South/West

ACCESS *Start from the vicinity of the Old Hill Inn. Lay-bys just above the pub. Station at Ribblehead on the Settle-Carlisle line, seasonal Sunday bus from Ingleton. •OPEN ACCESS - see page 8.*

The most famous mountain in the Pennines, and a favourite of all Yorkshiremen (and women), Ingleborough is a captivating hill. The manner in which it asserts itself, no more so than above Chapel-le-Dale, positively throws down a challenge: it wants to be climbed! Of the many ascent routes onto Ingleborough this is the shortest and easiest: a start at 1000ft above sea level contributes greatly to this.

Chapel-le-Dale is a scattered community on and around the Ingleton-Ribblehead road. The Hill Inn (properly the 'Old Hill') stands in isolation with 'the hill' in question, Ingleborough, rising spectacularly behind. The pub is immensely popular with hillwalkers and cavers, and a cracking atmosphere regularly prevails. The old school now serves as a bunkhouse. St Leonard's tiny church is all *but hidden in a cradle of foliage. It was restored in 1869, though some lovely mullioned windows remain. It also has an attractive little bell turret. Buried here were scores of victims from railway construction days at Ribblehead - mostly killed by disease.*

From the pub head up the road for 100 yards to a stile on the right, and rise to join a bridleway as it approaches a gate. Or, from the lay-bys above, drop towards the pub and take a gate on the left. At once Ingleborough's majestic stance fires the spirits, and a good track winds away past a well-preserved old limekiln, bound directly for the mountain. Through a gate a much gentler green way continues straight on through two further gates in walls between the lush

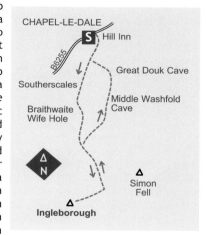

limestone pastures, and you enter Southerscales Nature Reserve of the Yorkshire Wildlife Trust. *This near-level first mile makes for a gentle warm-up and gives ample time to appraise the layout of this side of the mountain.* After a branch to Great Douk Cave goes left, a firmer track re-forms. Rising gently beneath a limestone scar, it swings up left to cross the edge of the Southerscales pavement. The track runs on past the massive sinkhole of Braithwaite Wife Hole to a pair of stiles onto the fell proper. This marks a sudden transition from limestone pastures to more austere, brown fellside.

At once a stone-flagged path takes up the running, and leads all the way up the moor towards the increasingly vertical-looking mountain wall which you must scale. At Humphrey Bottom the flags end abruptly at a wall corner, where a pitched path takes over. This winds steeply up, yet with relative ease to place you on the dramatic edge of the broad ridge running north to Simon Fell. A tiny stream is crossed to a kissing-gate to follow a broad path up the final slopes of Swine Tail. *Penyghent and Ribblesdale enter the scene to your left.* In the myriad rocks the stone-flagged Horton path merges and you emerge onto the tilted summit plateau. Despite the ease and condition of the paths thus far, if the clouds are down the plateau can bring navigational problems, particularly on leaving the top. Rising across it, however, the summit shelter appears in a couple of minutes, and is reached in a couple more.

At 2375ft/724m Ingleborough's summit is a place of great interest. The highest ground is occupied by a four-square wind shelter, complete with seating and incorporating a view indicator; an Ordnance Survey column; a massive, sprawling cairn between the two; and a great pile of stones nearer the Ingleton edge, ruins of a 'hospice' erected in 1830. Crumbling walls around the rim of the plateau are the remains of an Iron Age hill-fort of the Brigante tribes, and the bases of several hut circles can be discerned in the centre. As a viewpoint Ingleborough is supreme, with interest in all directions. Its position as a corner-stone of the Dales guarantees great variety of scenery: 'inland' is a skyline of rolling tops slotted in between Penyghent and Whernside, while far to the west are the Lakeland Fells; southwards are the Bowland moors, while the waters of Morecambe Bay glisten beyond Arnside Knott.

To leave, retrace steps off the plateau down to the kissing-gate, and re-cross the tiny stream just below it. *A fascinating alternative involving a steeper, rougher section of descent turns right on a broad path enjoying a classic traverse on a well-defined edge high above Humphrey Bottom to a stile in a wall: from here an initially steep descent eases to follow the wall down the moor*

to the corner, joining the main route. The main route returns down the pitched descent and back across the flagged moor to the wall. Without crossing, instead turn right on a lesser path that runs above the wall all the way along the moor-foot to the far end. Faced with two stiles take that in the wall ahead, from where a path crosses towards limestone outcrops at Middle Washfold Cave. *Here a small pavement and a solitary tree decorate the hole, which after rainfall swallows a sizeable stream. Alongside is an old stone sheepfold, while Ingleborough makes a fine backdrop.*

The path curves left in front of Middle Washfold, then on to a gate in a wall. Continuing away, it then bears right to approach the environs of Great Douk Cave, enclosed by a sturdy wall. *On the right just before it is the sinister-looking shaft of Little Douk Pot, accessed by a stile.* Curve round the outside of Great Douk's wall and go left to the bottom, where a stile gives access. A rough path drops into the massive hollow bedecked in trees. *At the top end a waterspout gushes enthusiastically out, to quickly seep innocuously below ground again. Alongside is the vertical, covered shaft of Great Douk Pot with fixed ladders descending eerily into the bowels of the earth.* Re-emerging, a broad way drops down to rapidly rejoin the outward route just a couple of fields from the end.

Opposite: Whernside from the summit

Ingleborough from the alternative return path

SMEARSETT SCAR

A beautiful walk through a limestone wonderland

START *Austwick (SD 767684; LA2 8BB)*

DISTANCE *5 miles (8km)*

ORDNANCE SURVEY 1:25,000 MAP
Explorer OL2 - Yorkshire Dales South/West
Explorer OL41 - Forest of Bowland & Ribblesdale

ACCESS *Start from the village centre. Roadside parking.
Ingleton-Settle bus.* •OPEN ACCESS - see page 8.

For a note on Austwick see page 38. From the green outside the pub turn down the narrow lane opposite, and quickly take a snicket on the right. Past the houses it emerges as a flagged path running through two fields to emerge onto the road on the edge of the village. Turn left to cross Austwick Bridge. *Here there is a good view to Moughton's flat top overtopping the cottages of Wharfe.* Immediately over, turn left along the walled track of Wood Lane. Where it bends left leave by a gate/stile on the right to cross the length of a field to a stile onto a walled bridleway to the right of enviably located Wood House. *Turning right would provide a stile-free route into Feizor.* Cross straight over the bridleway to climb the field opposite to a stile on the brow. *Pausing to appraise the view, Austwick nestles beneath the newly appeared flat top of Ingleborough, with its sidekick Simon Fell also well seen: Robin*

Proctor's Scar projects beneath Norber and its boulderfield. Ahead, meanwhile, Feizor is revealed beneath Pot Scar.

From the stile begin a generally obvious march through a string of stiles in this tidy block of fields with Oxenber and Feizor Woods on the left. *In early spring a riot of primroses decorate the base of this glorious traditional limestone woodland (visited later), while there are wide views over the Bowland moors to the right.* The stiles come thick and fast towards the end, maintaining a near-straight line to emerge into Feizor across a tiny beck. *Feizor is an unspoilt settlement at the terminus for motor vehicles of a short cul-de-sac to this hollow in the hills. Footpaths, however, radiate in all directions. Note the setted watersplash across the street with stone troughs alongside, and of more practical use, a splendid café to the left. A little beyond it is a lovely corner with a water pump and trough sat on a tiny green outside a row of cottages.*

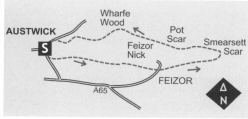

Go briefly left and leave by a stile on the right. Across a small enclosure you pass through a barnyard into a field. Ascend with the wall on your right to a stile near the top. *High to your left rises Pot Scar, a gleaming vertical wall of limestone and a favourite haunt of climbers.* Entering Open Access land, a super path continues the ascent through more colourful country, and when its groove fades Smearsett Scar is revealed ahead. Advance on through an old wall junction on the brow to a stile in a sturdy wall. Through another old wall the path crosses the edge of the upland hollow to approach a stile ahead. Before it, however, take a wallside path running left to a stile in a kink directly beneath Smearsett Scar. *Look back to see the intriguing 'Celtic Wall' on the skyline behind.* A thin path ascends the wallside to its brow, from where strike left up through the edge of the outcrops to attain the summit within five minutes.

At 1191ft/363m the top is occupied by an Ordnance Survey column, a scrappy pile of stones that was once a neat cairn, and three circular stone shelters. Partner of Pot Scar, Smearsett Scar boasts an arresting profile, particularly from the Stainforth area. Its south face falls away sharply, with low crags giving way to scree slopes. Its character is rivalled by its status as a viewpoint, and is probably the finest spot for appraising the newly-revealed Ribblesdale landscape. Included are Horton and Helwith Bridge backed by Plover Hill, Penyghent and Fountains Fell: then come Stainforth, its Scar, and Settle's inimitable hills. To the south are the 'Happy Valley' and the Celtic Wall with a distant Pendle Hill; northwards a tip of Whernside peeps around Ingleborough presiding over its limestone entourage. Pot Scar forms an enticing objective further along the undulating escarpment to the west....

Leave by heading west on an intermittent trod along the edge of the scarp, bound for Pot Scar: part way on, a scar deflects you 'inland'. *For a quicker continuation slant right down the pasture to pick up the Little Stainforth-Feizor Nick path at the edge of the field, passing through a gate/stile in the now sturdy wall and going left to Feizor Nick.* The more rewarding route keeps faith with the crest, so drop down a gap in the scarp and cross to the old wall, then rise on intermittent paths to the unmistakable crown of Pot Scar. At 1148ft/350m a massive pile of stones is surmounted by a circular shelter. *Just a short way beneath is the rim of the sheer limestone walls, over which climbers might suddenly appear. A nice feature of the panorama is the bird's-eye view of Feizor.*

A trod drops down to a stile in the wall just ahead, and runs on above further cliffs. It veers away from the declining edge, down to the start of a long, curving scar. Negotiate this and as the trod fades, bear right to meet the wall ahead: almost at once you encounter a sturdy stile built into it. *This reveals further lovely terrain of scattered trees and stony outcrops.* From the stile bear right towards the wall corner then cross to the Little Stainforth-Feizor Nick path, going left on it to a gate/stile onto the rough road through Feizor Nick. *During this stage omni-present Ingleborough has been usurped by enigmatic Penyghent across Ribblesdale.*

Turn right on it through a gate, but within yards go left to a stile into Wharfe Wood where a couple of excellent waymarked trails have been created. A path heads away on a meandering course through scattered scrubby trees, soon swinging left up to a clearing on a knoll. Here it bears right to almost merge with a wall on the left. With intermittent open views to Ingleborough the path gently declines into denser trees to arrive at a wall-stile in a corner. This puts you into Oxenber Wood, and the path drops into more open surrounds. Soon swinging left it rises gently to run through largely open terrain amid scattered limestone. Soon entering a vast, flat clearing, a junction of the two main paths is reached. Double back right, soon descending colourful open pasture.

Ahead is Wharfe beneath Moughton's tilted flat top, with Ingleborough dominant as ever ahead. Swinging right to drop down towards a clump of trees, the path then swings left beneath it and grandly down through bracken to a path and intake wall along the base. Go left on this through a gate/stile, and the green path drops down with the wall to a gate/stile at the bottom. Finally leaving Open Access land, a short-lived walled path drops down onto another walled way, Wood Lane again. Just a few paces left take a stile on the right, and descend the field to find a stile at the very bottom. This puts you onto a walled bridleway. Turn right to a ford at Flascoe Bridge. *This clapper bridge on Austwick Beck gives a splendid final moment.* Across, the way soon broadens out and runs on to the road on the edge of the village, going left to finish.

Moughton from above Austwick

CRUMMACK DALE

Easy rambling through peerless landscapes: simply gorgeous!

START *Austwick (SD 767684; LA2 8BB)*

DISTANCE *6 miles (9$\frac{1}{2}$km)*

ORDNANCE SURVEY 1:25,000 MAP
Explorer OL2 - Yorkshire Dales South/West

ACCESS *Start from the village centre. Roadside parking.
Ingleton-Settle bus. •OPEN ACCESS - see page 8.*

Austwick is a hugely attractive village set well back from the main A65 road. A small green, the cosy Gamecock Inn, a shop, an old hall, the tiny church of the Epiphany and countless cottages combine to create a scene of great charm. From the green outside the pub turn down the narrow lane opposite, and quickly take a snicket on the right. Past the houses it emerges as a flagged path through two fields to run along to the road on the village edge. Turn left to cross Austwick Bridge. *Here there is a good view to Moughton's flat top.* Across, turn left on the walled track of Wood Lane. Where it bends left leave by a gate/stile on the right to cross a long field to a stile onto a walled bridleway to the right of the enviably located Wood House. Cross straight over to climb the field opposite to a stile on the brow. *Pausing to appraise the view, Austwick nestles beneath the newly appeared flat top of*

Ingleborough, with its sidekick Simon Fell also well seen: Robin Proctor's Scar projects beneath Norber and its boulderfield. Ahead, Feizor is revealed beneath Pot Scar.

Heading away from the stile quickly leave the public footpath in favour of a hand-gate in the wall just to the left. This admits to Oxenber Wood, an area of Open Access. A waymarked path slants up through scattered trees to an old walled field now dense with bracken. From the top it ascends a little further to ease out on a brow. *Ahead is Moughton,*

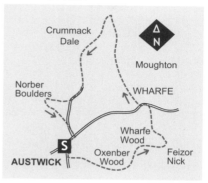

joined by Simon Fell and soon Ingleborough. The path runs delightfully on to a massive clearing, in the centre of which it forks.

Bear right, on between limestone pavements in a colourful, natural wonderland. *Penyghent makes a brief appearance.* On dropping down the path swings right, then with a branch dropping away, the waymarks confirm your route slants back right up to a hidden wall-stile. The path rises gently away through the denser Wharfe Wood, with a wall nearby on the right. A clearing is passed and the path reaches an open knoll. Having left the wall it drops faintly left before resuming the short way along to the right to an information panel and stile out of the wood. In front is the firm track through Feizor Nick. *Penyghent is magnificent across Ribblesdale.*

Turn left, but leave within a minute by a stile on the left. Drop to a gateway in the far corner, on the edge of Wharfe Wood. *Ahead, Wharfe itself nestles in the green bowl of Crummack Dale, beneath the limestone bulwarks of Norber and Moughton, and backed by Ingleborough flexing its broad shoulders.* Continue slanting down to another gateway, then down to a stile: a faint path drops to another stile in a parallel wall, finally level with the bottom corner of the wood. Advance to a stile ahead and cross a farm drive: the stream disappears as you cross the wall! From the stile behind cross the field centre to a stile, and over a footbridge on a lively stream to the next stile. Bear left across a larger field to a lesser bridge, with a stile onto the lane just further on.

Go left just a short way and at the bend take the enclosed old lane - a bridleway - to Wharfe. Swinging left to a fork bear right, slightly uphill, and the way runs on along the front of a house. *Amid a sea of late winter snowdrops, Beacon Light bears a 1726 date-stone.* Continue delightfully on to a tiny cottage, with the main grouping of Wharfe just below. *This improbable chocolate box hamlet hides from the outside world by leafy lanes that serve only as bridleways: the lovely Manor House is dated 1715.* Another bridleway rises from the hamlet and the way remains tightly enclosed as the narrowing White Stone Lane, and a wonderful ramble runs on past colourful verges. *High above are the gleaming limestone scars flanking Moughton, though some of your enclosing walls are composed of very different Silurian rock that is exposed across some of the fields here.* Rising gently past a couple of barns, leave by a stile on the right at a bend. Go left through a gateway into a vast pasture under Moughton's immensely colourful flanks. *Across lovely Crummack Dale, Ingleborough rises above Norber.*

A gentle green track heads away parallel with the lane, and on forking take the inviting right branch, straight up through a well-defined skyline nick. Just through this you reach a gate/stile behind what can be a lively stream after rain. Now cross two long fields with a stile linking them, at the end of the second ignoring a gate ahead in favour of a stile to the left to rejoin the lane. *During this spell isolated Crummack Farm is seen beneath Ingleborough, with Studrigg Scar directly above you and Moughton Scars ahead.* Turn right on the grassy lane's dead-straight course, opening out at a gate and on as far as a sharp bend. Here take a stile on the left and follow a wall doubling back to a simple footbridge on the sizeable Austwick Beck. Continue on the faint grassy way near the wall, all the way to a stile in a kink just short of the end.

Transferring to the other side of the wall resume as before, soon reaching a gentle brow amid Silurian slate outcrops. *Moughton looks impressive across the bowl of Crummack Dale.* Descend past the rocky wall to a corner stile, from where the path crosses a simple footbridge to three successive stiles to deposit you onto a junction of rough lanes. *Just before this note the fine example of a sheep creep on the right, passing beneath the walled Crummack Lane.*

Joining Crummack Lane on your right, follow its hard unsurfaced course left. *Reaching a brow there are grand views ahead to Smearsett Scar, Pot Scar, Wharfe Wood and Oxenber Wood.* The lane suddenly becomes surfaced and then absorbs a farm drive.

Just beyond, after it starts to descend, take a stile on the right and follow the wallside path rising away to approach Nappa Scars. After the first cliff pass through a stile in the old wall, then slant left to a stile accessing Norber boulderfield: these fascinating rocks are scattered everywhere! *The Norber Boulders are geological freaks, famous specimens of something the Ice Age brought in. A retreating glacier carried rocks from further up Crummack Dale and deposited them in their present position. What is so special is that they are dark Silurian rocks atop white limestone pedestals that have worn more rapidly away. They are termed 'erratic', and are a bit special.*

While your departure point is along to the left, for now follow the thin path rising away into the heart of the boulders. On easing out you can explore at will before bearing left, intermittent trods possibly guiding your steps across to pick up a broader green path just short of a prominent large cairn on a pile of stones. Turn left on this to drop down to a guidepost at a crossroads of paths. Drop right on the path that curves back left to follow a wall down to the bottom corner, where a small gate and stile await. Descend the fieldside, and part way along bear left to a gate/stile near the corner. Joining the enclosed track of Thwaite Lane, go left a few steps to a crossroads with Crummack Lane, and turn right to descend into Austwick.

At the Norber Boulders

GAPING GILL

A straightforward exploration of the many limestone features hidden in the fine valley above Clapham

START *Clapham (SD 745692; LA2 8EQ)*

DISTANCE *5³4 miles (9km)*

ORDNANCE SURVEY 1:25,000 MAP
Explorer OL2 - Yorkshire Dales South/West

ACCESS *Start from the village centre. National Park car park. Settle-Ingleton bus. Rail station a long mile distant on the Leeds-Morecambe line.* •*OPEN ACCESS - see page 8.*

Clapham is a beautiful village in a setting to match. It stands at the foot of Ingleborough from where Clapham Beck flows to form the village centrepiece, crossed by attractive bridges and lined by old cottages. Centrally placed are the New Inn, Post office, shops and cafes. By the car park is the Manor House with a 1705 lintel, and the Cave Rescue Organisation HQ. Just up the road is the church of St James with a 15th century tower. For many decades, into the 1990s, Clapham provided the cottage home for that revered Yorkshire magazine, the Dalesman. Near the church is Ingleborough Hall, currently an outdoor centre but formerly the home of the Farrer family. Best known of them was Reginald (1880-1920) who found fame as a botanist, collecting alpine plants on his journeys to far-flung parts and bringing many back to the *grounds of the hall. The heavily-wooded grounds and the lake were created by the family earlier in the 19th century.*

From the car park cross the road to a characterful stone-arched footbridge and take the road to the right. *Note an impressive waterfall plunging under an arched bridge in the estate grounds.* As the road turns left, pass through a gateway in front where a ticket machine collects your modest dues for entering the private grounds beyond. A broad path zigzags up to quickly reach the foot of the lake. Locked in glorious woodland, this ornamental lake is surprisingly extensive. This broad carriageway is followed the full length of the charming estate grounds.

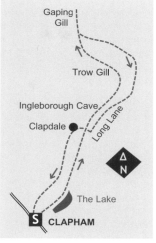

The drive climbs away from the lake, a sustained pull high above the tumbling beck to reach the Grotto. A short way beyond, you emerge into the open air of the upper reaches of Clapdale. With the flanks of Norber up to the right, the drive traces Clapham Beck along to Ingleborough Cave. *This is a showcave with guided tours: hot drinks are available here. Just past it a stone-arched bridge crosses the beck within yards of its birth. On the left here is Beck Head, from where the waters gush. The stream last saw daylight as Fell Beck, plunging into Gaping Gill: a connection by cavers was only established in the 1980s after many years' efforts.*

Over the bridge pass through a gate/stile and along a dry trough between low limestone scars. *On the bend, set back on the left at the base of a cliff is Foxholes, which has revealed evidence of Stone Age occupation.* The corner is rounded to pass through a gate/stile revealing Trow Gill just ahead, and your path climbs through it. *This former cave is now a dramatic, overhanging ravine, Gordale in style if not in proportions.* Emergence from the ravine is onto the open moor. *Little Ingleborough is quickly revealed, soon joined by Ingleborough itself.*

The path accompanies a wallside, ignoring an early stile and continuing along to reach a second stile. Just across it is Bar Pot. *This massive hollow is a popular cavers' route into the Gaping Gill system: mighty Ingleborough now totally dominates proceedings.* The path heads off across the virtually flat moor, initially still on limestone terrain. Within a few minutes a fork is reached, and the right branch leads after 150 yards to the unmistakable hollow that is Gaping Gill. *It will be clear from the outset that this is no place for skylarking or unrestrained children!*

Gaping Gill is the great hole, the one that everyone has heard of and that many non-cavers have descended. On the open moor in the lap of Ingleborough, this mighty chasm cannot fail to impress. The innocuous stream of Fell Beck suddenly plunges more than 330ft/100m from the unfenced lip to the floor of the chamber, which is said to be of sufficient size to hold York Minster. Over the Spring Bank and late Summer Bank Holiday weeks, local caving clubs set up a chair and winch to lower the likes of you and me into the depths - for a fee! Here several miles of passages radiate from the main chamber, and the course of Fell Beck finally returns to daylight as Clapham Beck, as already witnessed.

Having had a good - but cautious - potter around, retrace steps to the stile, then consider a more varied return making use of Open Access. Leaving the crowds behind take the inviting green path heading directly away. *It offers open views to Norber straight ahead, and more distantly Pendle Hill and the Bowland moors: very rapidly Penyghent glides smoothly into place for a time.* Initially gently, the path drops more markedly down, briefly fading a little as it drops towards a big grassy hollow. This contains a fenced shaft, and a now clearer way slants up to the right to point to a couple of gates. From the left-hand one you enter the head of Long Lane, a stony track which starts to drop away. *You could opt to remain on this all the way to a junction at the end, where turn right to drop back into the village.*

The best option involves a delve into and back out of Clapdale. Long Lane soon levels out to run parallel with Clapdale down below. Just as it starts a more gentle descent, with your objective of Clapdale Farm on the slopes opposite, take a stile and descend a wallside to a footbridge on Clapdale Beck by the entrance to the estate grounds. Bear right onto the driveway but leave within 100 yards by a gate/stile on the left, from where a broad path doubles back up the flank, climbing to Clapdale Farm. At the rear turn left through a gate/stile into its yard, then head away along its rough access road through the fields. *This gives good views across Clapdale to the broad plateau of Norber, with the Bowland moors ahead.* Descending to become enclosed and then later surfaced, it drops down to emerge onto a back road in the village. Go left to finish, ideally concluding by crossing the first bridge to approach the church, then turning right for the car park.

Opposite: Clapham

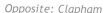

Bar Pot and Ingleborough

WATERFALLS WALK

A classic, and rightly so: don't come during a drought!

START *Ingleton (SD 693733; LA6 3ET)*

DISTANCE *4¹2 miles (7km)*

ORDNANCE SURVEY 1:25,000 MAP
Explorer OL2 - Yorkshire Dales South/West

ACCESS *Start from the Falls car park, reached down the steep road by the church. Bus from Kirkby Lonsdale and Settle. This walk is over private land, and requires payment at the start.*

The Waterfalls Walk has attracted visitors for over a century, and can be worth savouring in the winter months when free of jostling crowds. Though the paths are well-maintained, care is needed when wet leaves carpet the ground. Be also aware that for a low level walk, there is a fair amount of 'up and down' work. Refreshments are available at the start and en route. The valleys explored are remarkably alike, both the Twiss and the Doe being beautifully wooded and exposing fascinating geological features. The two becks meet in Ingleton to form the Greta. Ingleton itself is at the heart of Yorkshire's limestone country, and an ideal base for exploring the fells, scars and caves. The centre is dominated by a long-abandoned railway viaduct and St Mary's church. There are numerous pubs, cafes and shops, and also a youth hostel, climbing wall and swimming pool.

Few directions are needed as the paths are clear throughout. From the car park the path heads up the valley of the River Twiss, a lovely stroll through Swilla Glen passing a 'coin tree' and wood mushroom sculptures. It is some time before the first waterfalls are reached, the river being crossed twice to arrive beneath Pecca Falls, a delectable series of cataracts. Steeper work leads up past Hollybush Spout, emerging to pass a seasonal refreshment hut and into open country just short of the walk's highlight at Thornton Force. Few will not pause here to appraise this majestic single fall.

Resuming, the path zigzags up the side and around the glacial moraine of Raven Ray, where another bridge takes you up again to a corner gate onto Twisleton Lane. Turn right along its green course. *This highest point of the walk earns extensive views out to the Bowland moors.* Passing beneath Twisleton Scar End the way becomes surfaced to drop down to Twisleton Hall. Here keep left on a track above all the farm buildings, on through a gate/stile at the end. A path crosses a field and descends to a gate onto a back road. *Fine views to the majestic giant of Ingleborough entirely dominate this section of the walk.*

Cross straight over to Beezleys Farm, passing beneath the buildings and along to a seasonal refreshment centre. Drop down to Beezley Falls and follow the River Doe back downstream. Further features along this more gorge-like return leg include Rival Falls, a viewing platform high above Baxenghyll Gorge, the easily-missed Snow Falls, and this time just one crossing of the beck. Emerging from the trees, the path meanders on through scattered woodland and onto an open common. *Old quarry buildings are passed, with the final section enjoying an interesting prospect of the striking tilted rock strata in an old quarry across the beck.* Meeting a narrow road-end, this leads back along to the village centre.

Pecca Falls

KINGSDALE

*An intimate exploration of an unfrequented glacial valley
that brings geography colourfully to life: glorious views*

START *Thornton-in-Lonsdale (SD 692759; LA6 3PJ)*

DISTANCE *5½ miles (9km)*

ORDNANCE SURVEY 1:25,000 MAP
Explorer OL2 - Yorkshire Dales South/West

ACCESS *Start from the foot of Kingsdale. 1¾ miles on the Dent
road there is verge parking where Twisleton Lane turns off.
More parking before this point. •OPEN ACCESS - see page 8.*

*Kingsdale is a classic glaciated valley: uniform scars seam the
walls of the dale, and at its foot a moraine suggests a lake once
occupied the flat dale floor.* From the junction with Twisleton
Lane, head a few paces back in the Thornton direction to a stile on
the right. A thin trod climbs to a stile on the skyline, clambering
through limestone outcrops at the top. *Part way up, Ingleborough's
majestic form appears back over the valley.*

Initially curving left, the way climbs through more outcrops to
rise to a shelf with ruinous sheepfolds to your right. Up the small
gully behind, the outcrops recede as you emerge onto more open
pasture. *Ahead now is Gragareth, the fell on which your outward
route is walked.* Take a trod inclining half-right over much gentler
ground to close in on a sturdy wall, rising steadily but not actually

49

meeting the wall until the top corner. Here you also meet the Turbary Road at a wall junction.

Turn through the gate and head off in style along this superb old track, its harder surface soon giving way to a soft grassy base. The only thing to concentrate on now is ensuring most of the caves in the vicinity of the track are seen: some can't be missed. *'Turbary' is the right of us commoners to dig peat for fuel, and the road was built for the passage of carts to the Turbary Pasture higher up the fell. Today it serves as a splendid walkers' way, with a grand prospect of the bulk of Whernside and better still, a perfect springboard for inspection of the caves (or simply stay on the track!).*

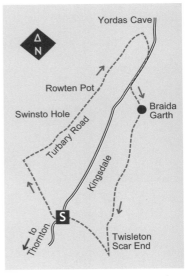

Strung along the limestone shelf occupied by the peat road, a magnificent series of caves and holes await inspection. Almost immediately through the first gate, Kail Pot is found 25 yards off-track in a uniform grassy hollow, a deep drop and the only one that is safely fenced. Pass through a gate ahead, ignoring a branch that curves right to another gate. *Up above, a long skyline leads on from Gragareth to Green Hill.* A parallel wall shadows you along to the next gate. Very quickly you reach the dry bed of a tiny stream, and followed left, within 150 yards it will guide you to Swinsto Hole. *This unassuming entrance to an important cave system is found just to the right.* Twin-like Suicide Pot and Blood Pot are passed on a slant back from Swinsto Hole to Turbary Pot, a tiny but distinctive hole alongside the track.

A further gate intervenes then it's quickly along to Rowten Pot. This is a visual feast, right on the path and appearing suddenly and dramatically. *Bedecked in vegetation, the irregular gaping chasm* drops no less than 350 feet/107m into the bowels of the earth. *Adjacent is a less obvious, more sinister hole. Across the path is the collapsed roof of Rowten Cave: 100 yards up the moor is the entrance, with the dry hole next to it offering a short adventure.* Immediately behind it a gate leads through sheepfolds, then you resume alongside a wall. Part way on, slant less than 100 yards up to where two trees conveniently mark the location of Jingling Pot. *This deep, vertical hole is bedecked with ferns and flowers and swallows a stream. Two covered shafts are passed en route to it.*

The track encounters one final gate, and the walls are left behind. Heading away, the track finally foregoes its level course to swing uphill, and here advance straight on a pathless course to quickly arrive at Bull Pot at the foot of a minor ravine. *This is another surprise: an innocuous slit proves to be a deep shaft with neat, fluted sides.* Now slant downhill towards the wall ahead. *Yordas Cave is in the trees ahead, while Ingleborough is about to disappear from view.* Pass through the modest (at this point) Shout Scar before doubling back down to a gate onto the road.

Turn right along the road for a few minutes until a stile on the left gives access to a footbridge over the dry, stony bed of Kingsdale Beck. *The normally subterranean beck re-surfaces at Keld Head, between your crossings of it.* Heading for the farm of Braida Garth, bear left to a prominent knoll, on which is a stile in the wall. A green track then passes a modern barn to join the farm drive. Go left up towards the house (the only habitation on the walk) but take a small gate on the right beneath it. Cross the small enclosure past the house to a stile out into a field beneath the bank of Braida Garth Wood. Head across this field and the next one to a stile beneath the end of the wood. *Over it is an old limekiln, and the start of a limestone scar above.*

A path slants up through dry reeds to a stile ahead (ignore a bridle-gate above), then head away with a wall. After a fence takes over and approaches a reedy tract, the path bears left across rough pasture to the next stile ahead. Continue to rise alongside a fence through a saddle ahead, with rounded Wackenburgh Hill to the right. After stiles in successive walls a green track is joined to descend to the cart track of Twisleton Lane. Double back right on this, which soon becomes enclosed (the Waterfalls path goes left) and runs down via a ford/footbridge on Kingsdale Beck and back to the start.

MIDDLETON FELL

An emphatic leg-stretcher encircling the wide open spaces of this unsung mountain: a real tonic on a clear day

START *Barbon (SD 628825; LA6 2LJ)*

DISTANCE *7$\frac{1}{2}$ miles (12km)*

ORDNANCE SURVEY 1:25,000 MAP
Explorer OL2 · Yorkshire Dales South/West

ACCESS *Start from the village centre. Car park at village hall.*
•OPEN ACCESS - see page 8.

   Unassuming Barbon nestles in a fine Lune Valley setting, tucked away at the foot of the Dales' westernmost fells. Features include St Bartholomew's church, the Barbon Inn, a cafe/shop, and an old Wesleyan chapel. Centrepiece is the war memorial on which the Shuttleworths of Barbon Manor are prominent. From the memorial leave the village by the road past the pub and the church, then turning left along the drive into Barbon Park. Across the bridge on Barbon Beck the drive swings right to climb to Barbon Manor, but keep straight on over the grass to pass the top end of a wood. From the gate at the end keep on to the buildings at Eskholme, then turn sharp right to ascend to a gate at the top. This is the last one until you pass back through it to finish the walk.
   The ascent begins in earnest with the first objective being the cairn on Eskholme Pike: a choice of routes awaits. Either make a

direct, steeper pull up short-cropped grass, passing on the way a natural stone chair, the slab of Devil's Crag, and a stone shelter: a thin trod forms part way up. A gentler route takes a grass quad track slanting left from the gate: when it runs left take the continuing slighter one ahead, slanting up the fell with ease to the base of stonier ground. It swings right here to rise as a thinner way, climbing to fade on a mildly stony shelf. From here bear right to cross to the big cairn on the rocky plinth of Eskholme Pike. *This prominent landmark well merits a halt to survey a super Lune Valley panorama.*

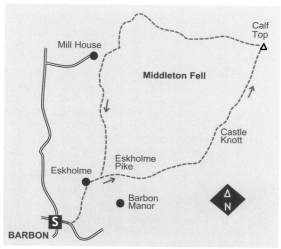

Behind the cairn a trod sets an obvious course along the crest of the grassy ridge, broadening into a quad track. Visible ahead is the cairn on Castle Knott, some way off and still some way short of the main summit. The slope eases further before a mildly stiffer pull, the path occasionally thinning slightly before gaining a tidy cairn. *The bulk of Great Coum looms ahead now across unseen Barbondale.* Passing above a clutch of tiny pools the path swings left beneath grassy knolls, and up ahead the top of Castle Knott beckons. A level section precedes the very short pull, noting an old stone sheepfold on a rash of stones across to the left. On gaining Castle Knott's cairn at 1765ft/538m, a surprise is in store in the form of a substantial depression interrupting the march to Calf Top, Middleton Fell's summit. *The environs of Castle Knott offer some dramatic views over Barbondale to Rise Hill, Baugh Fell, Widdale Fell and Great Coum, while more crucially your summit is at least now visible!* A briefly steep drop becomes slightly faint on the saddle, where a short moist section awaits. A peaty section amid heather precedes a grand pull on a broad path to gain the summit ridge. An old wall/fence corner is reached first, and it guides a simple stroll along to the Ordnance Survey column.

At 1998ft/609m Middleton Fell - or Fells, as the mass is known - is very much a detached parcel of upland. Few walkers venture here, thanks in part to its lack of (literally) inches. Resembling the Howgills in character, its slatiness is matched by its deeply incised western gills, its heather flanks, its isolation, and even its happy 'limitations' of altitude (despite which, up here you will feel exceedingly high and remote!). The summit, known as Calf Top, grants extensive views over the north-west counties: a step over the fence gives access to a contrasting close-up view down its sheer east flank. Westwards are Morecambe Bay and an extensive Lakeland skyline, northwards are Sedbergh and the Howgill

Fells, while closer still is Dentdale in its surround of sombre fells.

Whilst the obvious option is the pleasurable task of retracing steps (better in poor weather), consider a circular route. Bear west directly away from the summit over barely declining ground. Part way along this shoulder a broad grass track comes in from the right, and will remain your route all the way down to the intake wall. It runs past a small pool, over a slight rise and on to reveal a 7ft high stone pillar just 30 paces to the left. The track now commences a splendid descent with outstanding Lunesdale views, later entering scattered heather patches and maintaining a generally straight line down to a more defined edge, with a tiny cairn on a knoll to the right. The second half of the descent starts here, as the way drops a little more steeply but quickly fades: it can be picked up by dropping right to revive in a flatter, grassy area. Here it starts a level run to the right: you can soon short-cut this by dropping down alongside a tiny stream through sparse bracken. Within two minutes the track comes back from the right, crossing the stream and continuing as a mercurial green way slanting down the bracken-clad fellside. It takes you all the way to the base of the fell, only emerging from bracken two minutes above the intake wall.

Don't go right down to the wall but bear left to the foot of the tree-lined ravine of Millhouse Gill, beneath a super waterfall. Cross and rise briefly with the intake wall, then tramp a nice level course above the wall. As it drops away bear left to the top corner of a wall ahead. Continue atop this, with Eskholme Pike appearing ahead, and at the end a green path drops down into bracken. Veer left to contour across beneath the limit of the bracken, ignoring the lower intake wall and crossing over easy ground towards the plantation corner ahead. On past it, don't rush to join the wall but make use of sheeptrods on better terrain before gravitating towards the wall on good turf, soon reaching the gate back off the fell.

Waterfall,
Millhouse Gill

Opposite: Castle Knott

BANKS OF THE DEE

A simple riverside stroll of great charm and tranquillity

START *Dent (SD 704870; LA10 5QL)*

DISTANCE *4^{3}4 miles (7^{1}2km)*

ORDNANCE SURVEY 1:25,000 MAP
Explorer OL2 - Yorkshire Dales South/West

ACCESS *Start from the village centre, car park. Weekend Dalesbus. Dent Station on the Settle-Carlisle line is four miles distant.*

Dent is only a village in size, but is still known as Dent Town in recognition of a once greater importance. Today it is an unhurried backwater midway along its own valley: the only roads in and out are minor ones, a factor which has helped preserve some of Dent's character. Retained are cobbled streets lined with neat cottages, a Post office/shop, cafés and a pair of pubs. St Andrew's church dates in part from the 15th century: the tower dates from the late 18th century. Between the Sun Inn and the George & Dragon is a block of Shap granite serving as a drinking fountain, and carved with the name Adam Sedgwick. Born here in 1785, he spent over 50 years as Professor of Geology at Cambridge. One of the earliest and best in his field, he did much research into the fascinating geology of his own back yard. At least one of the pubs serves ale brewed just up the road in this very dale: support a local industry and savour an excellent product at the same time! Also here are a

Methodist church built as a Wesleyan Chapel in 1834, a Reading Room of 1880, a Zion Chapel of 1835 now serving as a meditation centre, while a heritage centre gives an excellent picture of the area in times past.

From the car park head along the cobbled street in the village centre, keeping left to drop down to Church Bridge. Don't use it but take a stile on the left to descend to the river. *Virtually at once there is a fine prospect of Dent Town under the slopes of Great Coum.* The Dee is hugged all the way to the walk's turning point, the footbridge at Ellers. The only breaks are early on, when the river nudges you onto a hundred yards of road, and approaching Barth Bridge, where gates take a more direct course onto the road. The riverbank path resumes across the road. *The crystal-clear Dee is in sedate mood, this outward bank being especially beautiful, backed by the colourful hollow of Combe Scar towering over the walk.*

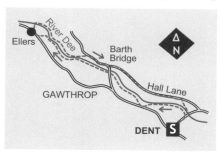

In a final tapering field, with the white cottage at Ellers ahead, the path is sent left across the field to a stile onto a back road. Go right on it the short way to the footbridge and ford by the cottage. Cross the bridge and set off back along the other bank, this lengthy section being entirely on the crest of a flood embankment. *Rise Hill fills the valley side to the left, with Whernside ahead.* At the end a wooded bank forces you up onto the road at a monument. *The Elam Monument is a tablet honouring one Lucy Elam, who in 1876 footed the bill for a re-routing of this section of road.* Turn right to quickly arrive back at Barth Bridge. *To savour more of the riverbank cross and retrace the opening mile.* For the circular route, remain on this bank along Hall Lane. This gem of a traffic-free way is wrapped in delightful hedgerows, initially by the river. Shortly after passing the attractive, white-walled Low Hall, a stile returns you to the grassy riverbank for the final field back to steps and a stile up onto Church Bridge.

FLINTER GILL

Beckside and fellside walking combine to give delightful close-hand and majestic distant views over Dentdale

START Dent (SD 704870; LA10 5QL)

DISTANCE 5½ miles (9km)

ORDNANCE SURVEY 1:25,000 MAP
Explorer OL2 - Yorkshire Dales South/West

ACCESS *Start from the village centre, car park. Weekend Dalesbus. Dent Station on the Settle-Carlisle line is four miles distant.*

For a note on Dent see page 56. From the car park cross the road and take one rising away past the school. A delightful group of cottages precede the start of Flinter Gill. *On the left is a former Zion Chapel of 1835.* At the last cottage the stony track of Flintergill Outrake takes over to climb above the beck. *In this enchanting setting, Flinter Gill tumbles over a series of rock ledges in a deep, wooded ravine, though after a dry spell the beck may be conspicuous by its absence.* Features of interest punctuate what is a steep and stony climb. *Immediately on the left are the Dancing Slabs, a flat shelf of rock used by local weavers for dampening and trampling on their cloth to improve it! This is followed by the Wishing Tree. Higher, a gate on the right gives access to High Ground Farmstead, a barn containing a small museum of farming implements. Back on route you pass a restored limekiln with a small quarry behind.*

Near the top of Flinter Gill the way emerges from its wooded confines and the gradients finally ease out. A stile on the right just before a gate gives access to a modern toposcope which details the magnificent view. *On parade is a great sweep of Dentdale leading down to the Howgill Fells across the foot of the valley.* Largely enclosed by walls but easier under-foot, the way rises to quickly join an enclosed track, the Occupation Road. *If you didn't visit the toposcope, then a most beautiful scene awaits as lower Dentdale leads the eye to the grouping of the Howgills.*

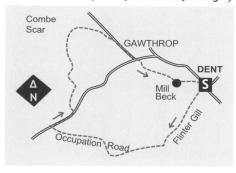

The Occupation Road runs across the northern flank of Great Coum, linking the Dent-Ingleton road with that from Dent to Barbon. An old packhorse way and service road for the enclosures, it provides marvellous sweeping views over the dale. Turn right along its wide course for a long, elevated stride. Soon reaching a high point at around 1180ft/360m, the way gradually curves around and down to eventually meet the Dent-Barbon road.

Accompany the road briefly right, rising gently to its summit at around 985ft/300m on Stone Rigg. *Looking back, Great Coum forms a long, flat skyline.* From a gate on the left a grassy track heads diagonally away, keeping left of profuse limestone outcrops to a ladder-stile in the far corner. From it a rougher track heads left with an old wall towards the steep slope, and while a quad track scales the slope, a firmer track swings right across a scrubby bank. *This superb promenade gives massive views up the dale, featuring Dent Town itself: Baugh Fell looms over the shoulder of Rise Hill ahead.* From a gate at the end the super green way continues, enclosed, to Combe House. *This shelters beneath the striking hollow of Combe Scar, a colourful scene chiselled out of the northern flank of Middleton Fell: a popular Dentdale landmark, its low crags give it more then a hint of Lakeland.*

Follow the rough drive dropping away, and as it winds down through old walls, forsake it for a path making a bee-line for the buildings at Tofts. A tiny footbridge on a tree-lined beck precedes steps up the opposite bank. Through a small gate pass between the buildings and out on the drive, to be rejoined by Combe House drive. The track drops gradually down past Bower Bank to a back road at Underwood. Gawthrop is just a few level minutes to the right, a picturesque group of cottages and farms well off the beaten track.

At the junction advance straight on over the bridge, and as the road drops steeply away take the last drive on the right at some seats. This access road swings left between houses to bridge a beck. Go straight ahead, left of Gawthrop Hall and on a concrete drive. As it swings sharp right uphill, take a gate in front of a short row of cottages and a briefly enclosed green way runs to a barnyard. Pass through and head along the top of two sloping fields, through stiles and rising gently through the next field centre to a gateway on a brow. With the village revealed ahead, advance to a gate by a seat, and descend a track to the farm complex at Mill Beck.

Remain on the main track the full length of the buildings and out into a field at the end. Drop left to the right-hand of two corner gates, and cross a field bottom to a stile in front of a large modern barn. Pass to its left alongside a caravanners' field at High Laning Farm. Head right towards the yard, then out along its drive to emerge onto the road through Dent by the Methodist Chapel of 1834.

Dent from Flinter Gill

DEEPDALE

A delightful excursion deep into a peaceful side valley with glorious views over Dentdale too

START Dent (SD 704870; LA10 5QL)

DISTANCE 5 miles (8km)

ORDNANCE SURVEY 1:25,000 MAP
Explorer OL2 - Yorkshire Dales South/West

ACCESS Start from the village centre, car park. Weekend Dalesbus. Dent Station on the Settle-Carlisle line is four miles distant.

For a note on Dent see page 56. From the car park head along the cobbled street in the village centre, keeping left at the George & Dragon to drop to Church Bridge. *Across the valley is Rise Hill, up the dale rises Whernside, while back over the village is Great Coum.* Don't cross the bridge but take a path on the right and head away upstream, immediately deflected from the Dee by Keld Beck. Follow this just as far as a farm bridge on it, across which cross to a wall just ahead and then bear right with this as it guides a path curving back to the river. Simply head upstream on a largely enclosed path that faithfully shadows the enchanting Dee. Keep straight on the riverbank at a junction with a bridleway at a ford and stepping-stones. *Ahead, mighty Whernside encloses Deepdale.*

Two minutes beyond the ford is a major confluence with Deepdale Beck. *This lovely spot deserves a pause: the side beck can often be entirely dry here.* Deepdale Beck - or at least its deep course - is now your companion all the way to Mill Bridge, where you emerge via trees onto a road. Go left over the bridge and rise away outside a plantation to quickly reach a fork. Take the narrow 'no through road' branching right at a tiny Methodist chapel, the entrance to Deepdale.

Deepdale causes the only real break in Dentdale's steep valley sides. Deepdale Beck flows for no more than three miles in its entirety, but it creates a deep-cut side valley which is very much a chip off the old block. It might even be said to be less spoiled than Dentdale, if that's possible. Its farms are dotted about the lush pastures in what appears to be a virtual time capsule. The Methodist chapel stands in a typically isolated location embowered in trees, while nearby Whernside Manor was built about 200 years ago.

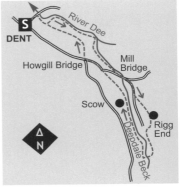

The road, Dyke Hall Lane, climbs away to reveal Deepdale outspread. Levelling out as the enclosed track of the Craven Way turns off left, within a minute you also leave by a gate on the left. *You could opt to remain on this traffic-free road as the route rejoins it further along.* Bear right across an unkempt pasture, slanting above a stone hut and on through a line of gnarled trees. Continue slanting up to a stile in a short length of wall near the top. Advance across a more welcoming field-top to approach Rigg End. *Great Coum now appears massive above Deepdale's fields. Looking back down-dale are the Howgill Fells, with the nearer Combe Scar to the left and Rise Hill to the right.*

Pass along the front outside the farm, crossing the drive and across to a gate in the wall ahead. Head directly away, dropping slightly to a wall-stile ahead. *A complete Deepdale horseshoe now features Pike, Whernside, White Shaw Moss, High Pike, Green Hill and Great Coum.* Drop down through a gateway to rejoin the road, now merely a concrete track. *On your left stands an old limekiln.*

Turn right down the now enclosed road just as far as a sharp bend right. Leave by a gateway on the left, crossing the field-top to a stile in a tiny section of wall above a wooded bank of Deepdale Beck. From a stile at the end of the trees drop down across a large, sloping pasture, crossing a small stream midway and continuing on to a stile in a tiny section of wall beneath a barn. Cross a single-slab bridge behind and from a kissing-gate advance on to a stile and a tiny, tree-lined stream. This time slant down the field to Bigholme Bridge, a farm bridge on the beck. *Deepdale Beck flows musically over broad limestone slabs.* Across, ascend a rough track by the fence to a corner gate just above. Through this you turn to begin a long march downstream along the valley. Head away, on through two further gates from where a wall guides the old way along to a barn. While a path branches up to the left, take the briefly enclosed green way curving down to the beck, another lovely spot.

Ignoring an inviting footbridge, remain on this bank and head off downstream, commencing a lengthy section close by the lively beck. Passing through a wall-stile immediately beneath the farm of Scow, quickly bear left of a small plantation to leave the beck. Bear slightly left to a path junction at a stile, behind which is a limekiln. Advance on by a scrubby bank and rise slightly to an old stile ahead, then cross a longer pasture to a kissing-gate in a sturdy wall. Through this advance on to a corner gate to join a back road. Go left on this past cottages and Cage Farm, rising sharply to a road junction. *The seat here enjoys massive Dentdale views, from Widdale Fell down to the Howgill Fells. Just beyond is Howgill Bridge.*

Leave the road at this junction by the enclosed cart track of Double Croft Lane, descending to this idyllically-sited eponymous house. While the bridleway advances on to meet your outward riverbank path, your way takes a stile on the left just before the house. Cross to a stile beyond it, and advance on a briefly enclosed green way. Through a gate at the end continue on with a hedge on your left, and keep on to a stile at the very end. From here a clear path shadows a tiny beck through scrub, leaving by a stile just before the end. In front a gate/stile point to a ford/stepping-stones on the larger Keld Beck just above, but your way takes the adjacent stile and crosses to one in the corner just beyond. Here a good enclosed path shadows Keld Beck back to the farm bridge near the start. Cross it and retrace opening steps back to Church Bridge, just ahead.

GARSDALE

A modest stroll through farmland and by a lovely riverbank

START *Garsdale Foot (SD 694912; LA10 5NU)*

DISTANCE *6¹2 miles (10¹2km)*

ORDNANCE SURVEY 1:25,000 MAP
Explorer OL2 - Yorkshire Dales South/West (tiny section)
Explorer OL19 - Howgill Fells/Upper Eden Valley

ACCESS *Start from the large Longstone Common car park, 2¹2 miles out of Sedbergh where the Hawes road becomes unfenced.*

   Garsdale is today probably the least known of any valley in the National Park - certainly for its size - though Norse settlers knew it well enough. Leave the car park by the minor road that drops to cross the River Clough at Danny Bridge, and this traffic-free byway leads up-dale for a good mile and a half. After a steep initial pull, bear right at an unsigned fork. Several farms are passed and several gates are met.

   Eventually, after a short, steep pull just beyond Lindsey Fold Farm on a sharp bend, take a drive on the left labelled Bellow Hill. Follow it over a dome as far as the first gate, but then turn right along the wallside to a corner stile. *Up behind is Baugh Fell, a mighty hill that dominates the walk.* Continue on with the wall, later veering right to a stile and tiny stream. Now cross to a stile ahead just above the house at Pike Hill. Turn down the drive out onto the main road, and go left with care for a swift quarter-mile.

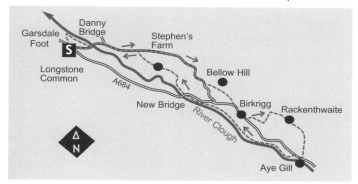

Just past the house at Birkrigg take a stile on the left and follow the wall away to a driveway. Turn left up this to a farm, rising right of it on a green way to a barn above. Pass along the front and out into a field, crossing beneath the wall to a stile/stream, and on again to a wall-stile. Keep on through a gate behind, and across to the right of farm buildings at West Rackenthwaite to join the drive. Ignore a wall-stile in front and turn up it to the house, along the front to a stile into a sloping field. Slant down to a gate just short of the end to join the East Rackenthwaite drive just behind. Again go left up towards the yard, but take a gate to the right of the first barn. Head across the field to find a wall-stile part hidden beyond scrub, then slant down to a small gate in the next wall. Now drop right to a gate behind a house, taking the left-most gate and down the house side. From a gate in front a nice enclosed pathway drops into trees, swinging right at the bottom and along to a gate back onto the main road opposite a stone-arched bridge at Aye Gill.

Turn right for less than a minute to a stile on the left, and cross the field centre towards the river. A gate and small stream precede a stand of trees keeping you briefly away from the Clough, but from a stile at the end you are firmly planted on the riverbank for the entire way back to New Bridge. *Close by a farm bridge there are glimpses of the splendid white-walled, mullioned windowed Swarthgill House.* Squeezing through narrow sections here leads to big sweeping pastures. Further, a stile puts you up onto a driveway at another farm bridge. Though you don't cross it, the shell on your left across is a tiny former Wesleyan Methodist Chapel. Follow the drive briefly to where it turns right for the adjacent road, and here pass through a gate to retain the riverbank for the final pasture, before a stile sends an enclosed section to the road at New Bridge.

Cross and take steps on the left down to a plank bridge, and a grass track heads downstream as far as the field end. Here turn right on the track away from the river to reach a corner gate. Approaching a barn, rise to its right to find a gate directly behind it. Rise gently to a wall-stile opposite, and head off across several field bottoms (stiles), dropping to a tiny stream crossing before a gentle rise to Stephen's Farm ahead. Pass along the front of the buildings to a gate in the facing wall at the end, and with Hole House Farm ahead, bear right to a corner gate. A brief enclosed way runs on to the farm. Head straight on past the buildings and follow the short drive out onto the road on which you began.

Go left to retrace steps to Danny Bridge, and for a variation

finish, across it take a path to the right to enjoy some of the Sedgwick Geological Trail. This traces the hugely attractive river downstream, with several marker posts indicating various geological features. After around 15 minutes plum on the bank is a cave looking over a lovely little waterfall. Just past it the faint path rises a little to a brow looking down on the calmer river downstream. From this point it is easiest to rise slightly to locate a slight sunken path rising to the left, doubling back to lead most of the way back to the car park just above.

River Clough

WINDER & CROOK

*The southernmost tops of the Howgills form a splendid
introduction to the group on some delightful paths*

START Sedbergh (SD 658921; LA10 5AD)

DISTANCE 4 miles (6^{1}2km)

ORDNANCE SURVEY 1:25,000 MAP
Explorer OL19 - Howgill Fells/Upper Eden Valley

ACCESS Start from the town centre. Car parks.
Infrequent bus links with Kendal, Kirkby Stephen and Dent.
•OPEN ACCESS - see page 8.

Sedbergh is the largest community in the Dales National Park,
yet its isolation has helped it avoid the excesses of commercialism.
Ceded to Cumbria in 1974, Sedbergh was previously in the north-
western extremity of the West Riding of Yorkshire, over 100 miles
distant from Sheffield. This tiny market town boasts a peerless
setting on the lower slopes of the Howgill Fells, with three lively
rivers, the Dee, Clough and Rawthey joining forces to swell the
waters of the nearby River Lune. Sedbergh is dominated by its
public school founded in the early 16th century. Other features of
interest on or near the lengthy main street include St Andrew's
church with a 15th century tower, and other parts dating back to
Norman times. Sedbergh is also making ambitious strides as
England's 'Book Town', an admirable asset that dovetails with the
peaceful ambience of the locality.

67

Leave the main street by Joss Lane rising past the main car park. It swings right and along to leave suburbia at a gate where an access road takes over. Here take the track slanting left to the top corner of the field, with your two fells waiting conveniently above. Ignore the track's left turn and take a corner stile, from where an enclosed path climbs away. It emerges to rise delightfully above tree-lined Settlebeck Gill, and at the top the open fell is gained at an iron kissing-gate. With a choice of paths, take the less obvious one, running down to ford the beck above a waterfall.

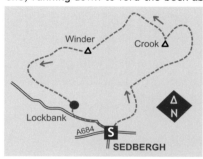

Vague paths ascend to a wall corner just above. From here rise just a few paces to locate the start of a green path sloping to the right, through a few reeds then into bracken across the face of Crook. So begins an impeccably graded promenade that only ever cautiously gains height. *Big views look over Garsdale to Widdale Fell, Whernside and Great Coum, and as you progress, Baugh Fell dominates across Rawtheydale. Just ahead are the neighbouring lower Howgills summits of Sickers Fell and Knott.* Soon after swinging round high above the deep enclave of Ashbeck Gill, you pass through a small rash of stones, just beyond which, with Arant Haw ahead, a fork is reached. Though the onward route is temptingly dead-level, you should trace one of the sunken ways climbing left: from the top of the left option a trod continues on easier ground above, though this is also easily gained from the more slanted right option. Either way you quickly arrive on easier ground on the ridge descending from Arant Haw, and doubling back left the summit of Crook will be quickly gained.

At 1509ft/460m, Crook's top features a substantial cairn on a plinth of short-cropped grass. Sweeping views look over Garsdale and the Rawthey backed by Wild Boar, Swarth and Baugh Fells, while westwards are Morecambe Bay and the Lakeland Fells, and more importantly, partner Winder! The cairn overlooks a steeper faced little alp across a miniature saddle containing a stone shelter.

68

Leave by a slightly wider path running north-west, left of the alp and dropping steeply off it to level out and quickly fork. Keeping left, you can see your way heading for the start of the slopes rising towards Arant Haw. At an early cross-paths keep on, undulating along while barely gaining height, to reach the reedy beginnings of Settlebeck Gill. Across it advance a minute further to another path crossroads: take the broader one left, commencing a brief steady descent to quickly merge into the broad Sedbergh-Calf bridleway.

Turning your back on the higher Howgills, drop left on this, and ignoring any branches it levels out to make an easy ascent over this broad ridge's grassy knolls to Winder's summit. At 1551ft/473m it is crowned by an Ordnance Survey column and a topograph. *The superb panorama includes a fine prospect up to the Lune Gorge and less frequented western Howgills. Garsdale and Dentdale are particularly appealing as they burrow deep into the higher fells of the Dales. Drop a little towards Sedbergh for an intimate bird's-eye picture, a fitting scene as Winder is the town's 'special' fell.*

Leave by a path striking west towards the Lune, the initial few strides less obvious but then becoming a clear green way. This descends with increasing style and remarkable rapidity to within a few paces of the intake wall. Turn left to find a slim path crossing a couple of small streams, then contouring on through bracken above the wall as Sedbergh appears ahead. As the bracken ends a quad track is joined, slanting down to meet the wall then dropping to the bottom corner, where a gate accesses the rear of Lockbank Farm. A short green way drops into the yard, then down the farm drive to emerge onto Howgill Lane, turning left to finish.

Settlebeck Gill

BRIGFLATTS & DENT FOOT

*A delightful stroll by riverbank and gentle
pastures where the Rawthey and Dee merge*

START *Sedbergh (SD 658921; LA10 5AD)*

DISTANCE 5½ *miles (9km)*

ORDNANCE SURVEY 1:25,000 MAP
Explorer OL2 - Yorkshire Dales South/West (tiny section)
Explorer OL19 - Howgill Fells/Upper Eden Valley

ACCESS *Start from the town centre. Car parks.
Infrequent bus links with Kendal, Kirkby Stephen and Dent.*

For a note on Sedbergh, see page 67. Go west on the main street to the church and turn down the Dent road, quickly taking a path right between the churchyard and Sedbergh School's cricket pitch. *This famous public school counts many famous names amongst its old boys, one of the best known being record-breaking England rugby caption Will Carling.* Meeting a track at the end, bear left on a still surfaced path along the back of the pavilion. Cross over a drive to a kissing-gate into a field, and with the frontage of the school to the right, head straight down to a kissing-gate onto a road. Cross straight over and away on a track past more sports fields. Reaching a barn take a kissing-gate on the right, and a path crosses to the field's far end. Curving round beneath a lone house, keep straight on past it to a kissing-gate onto a narrow lane.

Go left past attractive cottages at Birks, but on the bend beyond them take a kissing-gate on the right and bear left to a wall corner. Keep on the wallside to a kissing-gate at the far end, straight on a further field, then bear right to a pair of gates flanking a track. Continue to an underpass in the railway embankment ahead. *To the right this transforms into a cutting to approach Sedbergh's station on this former Clapham-Lowgill branch line.* Through it, bear left to the left-hand of two gates in a wall, then on through two fields to neatly emerge into the Quaker hamlet of Brigflatts. *Opposite is a Quaker burial ground, while just to the left in the beautiful setting of this former weaving hamlet is an historic Friends' Meeting House. Incorporating a 1675 datestone, it is one of the oldest Quaker establishments in the country, and still put to its original use. If it is open take a few respectful minutes to view the atmospheric interior, and perhaps leave a donation.*

High Brigflatts, opposite, bears a lintel dated 1743.

Return along the access road out onto the A684, and go left for a few minutes as far as a kissing-gate on the left. An enclosed path doubles back to run above a

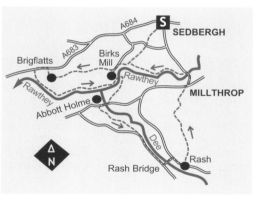

wooded bank of the Rawthey, dropping down at the rear of Brigflatts Farm to join the river in open pasture. With superb river scenery this leads unerringly to Birks Mill. *Additionally you encounter an old railway bridge, with the old line giving good views to Winder and the nearest Howgill Fells, and also the delightful tree-shrouded confluence with the inflowing River Dee.*

At Birks Mill, a former cotton-spinning mill, cross the Rawthey by a high footbridge on a lovely section of the river. Up the small bank opposite, turn downstream. From a corner stile the path runs through the woodland of Elysian Shades, quickly climbing to a small gate out of the trees. With the river gone, the thin path heads away to another gate just ahead: in front is Holme Fell. Emerging onto Sedbergh golf course, watch for flying balls and bear right, crossing to a broad gap in a hedge, then continue to a gate/stile onto a back road. Go briefly right to Abbott Holme Bridge, across which take a stile on the left. This admits to another section of the course. *This time be wary of balls flying from the left: here the sportsmen must hit their ball over the River Dee, or forfeit it to the waters! This is another lovely section of river, the Dee passing beneath its shapely final bridge prior to joining the Rawthey.*

Head upstream, quickly escaping the golf course at a stile. Beyond a tiny stream the route bears left, rising steadily along a scant row of trees. At the end is a stile into rougher pasture, and a path slants gently up the steepening bank above the river to a small gate in the wall at the top. *This is a fine moment as Dentdale is revealed ahead, yet with all earlier features still present: the river is backed by the Howgills, Wild Boar Fell, Swarth Fell, Baugh Fell, Rise Hill, Whernside, and Combe Scar overlooking lower Dentdale.*

A delectable green way heads off above a dense bracken bank, tracing the wall all the way to eventually reach a stile onto another back road. Go left on this traffic-free way, the surroundings of the nearby river remain idyllic. The first buildings reached are an old mill with millstones still lined up outside, and the humble Dent Foot Methodist Chapel. At Rash Bridge just beyond, cross the river and climb to the Dent road. Go right to the farm buildings of Rash, en route passing a milestone advising the distance to Sedbergh. Take a gate on the left and a thin path climbs to a wall-corner, continuing up to a gate/stile: this is the only real climb of the walk. Continue up the next field, bearing left to find a stile at the very top corner onto a lovely green bridleway. Go left, and at an early fork remain on the top one which soon swings right to the brow. *This high point of the walk trades Dentdale for the Rawthey scene once more, as Sedbergh and the Howgill Fells return to view.*

A bridle-gate admits onto the old golf course. Take the path straight ahead, crossing a track which is soon rejoined and then followed away. This drops more steeply with a wall, becoming a stony lane to descend into Millthrop. Turn right through the hamlet to a T-junction. *This tiny, tightly-packed settlement features an attractive terrace of old millworkers' cottages and a curiously-shaped Methodist chapel of 1889, with one of 1888 next door: both are now houses.* Go left at the junction to drop back onto the Dent road by the Rawthey, just short of Millthrop Bridge.

Across, take a small iron gate after a drive on the left. Bear right across the field to a stile into a wood at the end. Remain on the left-hand path above a steep drop to the river. Soon reaching another fork, the right branch leads through an intriguing walled sunken section. Emerging, take the right-hand of two paths going left, quickly leaving the wood at a kissing-gate. Go left with the fence past the wood corner to a ruined folly on a brow. *Winder fronts the ever-enticing prospect of the Howgill Fells.* Drop down the field towards the Rawthey and head downstream past a sports field. The path rises towards the lone house encountered early in the walk. From here turn right to retrace opening steps into town.

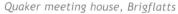

Quaker meeting house, Brigflatts

THE CALF SKYLINE

*Outstanding green pathways on typical Howgills slopes
present a magnificent circuit over the crown of the fells*

START *Howgill (SD 633950; LA10 5HZ)*

DISTANCE *7^{1}2 miles (12km)*

ORDNANCE SURVEY 1:25,000 MAP
Explorer OL19 - Howgill Fells/Upper Eden Valley

ACCESS *Start from Howgill church, 2^{3}4 miles on Howgill Lane out
of Sedbergh, in a hollow behind a gated road. Thoughtful parking
alongside. A donation in the church collecting box would be a
nice gesture for use of the verge. •OPEN ACCESS - see page 8.*

Dating from 1838, the little church of the Holy Trinity beside
Chapel Beck is the heart of Howgill's scattered farming community.
Back on Howgill Lane turn left over the bridge, and steeply uphill
to the farm at Gateside: already the day's skyline is evident to the
right. From a stile on the right before the farm, head on to the end
of the buildings then bear left to a corner gate. Just above, join a
track bearing right and swinging in to fade as it bridges a tiny stream.
Rise up the steep slope in front to find a stile in a wall at the top,
then slant right beneath a small stand of trees to a small corner
gate above. *This reveals the full promise of your walk, with the
high Howgills ridge ahead.* Drop briefly with the wall on your left,
and through a gate in it a track rises left to Castley Farm.

Ascend the driveway between the buildings to a track junction at the top. While the drive turns left your way is right, the enclosed cart track rising again before leveling out for a grand stroll along to a gate onto the open fell. The track drops slightly right to head off towards the hills, slanting down above Long Rigg Beck to drop to a ford on it. *A fantastic sense of remoteness pervades in this lovely spot.* The track fords the beck to commence the long and uncomplicated ascent of White Fell. Initially steep and rough, stay on the main track which improves to rise ever more delightfully up this broad spur. *To your left is distinctive Fell Head, with Bram Rigg Top and Calders in front and Arant Haw over to the right: ironically it is only The Calf itself which remains hidden until much higher. Several grooved sections add to the delights, as do views back to a long skyline of the Lakeland Fells.*

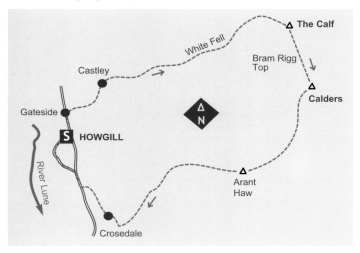

Higher, the path slants right in a splendid groove, looking down on the deep upper reaches of Calf Beck. *The Three Peaks appear in unison far across to the right, while the gleaming white trig. point of The Calf also appears, happily much nearer than the very distinctive looking Penyghent and Ingleborough!* As the going eases keep to the main right path above the steeper slopes falling right, contouring around and doubling back right to confirm its goal of The Calf. Passing beneath the minor highest point of White Fell Head, the path merges with the Fell Head-Calf path from the left for the final short pull to the waiting Ordnance Survey column.

At 2218ft/676m this marks the summit of the Howgill Fells. The Calf's plateau, however, restricts its views to distant lines of the Cross Fell group in the North Pennines, and the widely spread hills of the Dales to east and south. On a clear day the serrated Lakeland skyline to the west will claim most attention beyond a Lune Valley foreground; Morecambe Bay is also well seen. A cairn stands across the main path, with an often-dry pool beyond. Leave by bearing right on the firm Sedbergh path, dropping to a minor depression then rising onto the shoulder of Bram Rigg Top, whose minor summit at 2204ft/672m is just across to the right. The main path continues south to very quickly reach the cairn on Calders. *At 2211ft/674m this superbly sited summit is a fine vantage point on the edge of a more pronounced drop than The Calf.*

From the adjacent fence corner the broad path swings right, descending steeply to the saddle of Rowantree Grains. Improving underfoot as it goes, the fence is left behind to rise briefly to a shoulder of Arant Haw. Just short of the brow leave the main path for a much thinner one that bears gently right up and along to Arant Haw's summit cairn at 1985ft/605m. *This stage enjoys grand views to the right of the western cirque of high Howgills, from Fell Head around to Calders. More distantly, the long Lakeland skyline features Black Combe, the Coniston Fells, the Scafells and Great Gable, with the Helvellyn group over Ill Bell and High Street.*

Resume westwards to commence the descent on a delightful little path down the gentle ridge. Reaching a saddle in front of a minor knoll the thin path forks. While the right branch surmounts the knoll, your way is the left one, briefly contouring before resuming the descent onto the south-westerly spur of Nab. The intermittent path crosses its top before beginning the steeper final section, now a thin but clear trod. Deflected left by a wall corner, a track is met above Crosdale Beck. Before it passes through a corner gate off the fell, instead drop left to a ford on the stream by sheep pens. *The stream crossing makes for a pleasant final linger, with aggressively rocky walls immediately downstream.* A rough track slants up the other side, keeping right to very quickly find a gate off the fell.

Don't advance to the cottage at Craggstone, but head down the enclosure to a small gate into trees above the stream, noting a splendid waterfall. The thin path drops to a footbridge on Crosdale Beck then slants up to Crosedale Farm just above. Go left through the yard, but level with the house on the left, pass through a small gate onto its drive. Head right on this, but within a few strides leave through another small gate ahead. Cross straight over an access track to a gate from where a farm track heads off with a hedge. It runs on through a second field to an odd arrangement of gate and stile at a stream crossing. After a briefly enclosed section, head away along the right side of the field, passing through a gate midway to resume on the other side of the wall. A gate at the end puts you onto an enclosed farm track: go left onto Howgill Lane.

Turn right as far as a crossroads with Birkhaw drive, and for a varied finish, take the meandering back road to the left. *Up to the right, enjoy a fine picture of these western Howgills.* Ignoring all branches left, the road winds round to drop down to Mill House. *The former mill stands alongside: note the long-dry water cut that once supplied the waterwheel at the mill from Chapel Beck.* The church, and thus the finish, also appears just ahead.

White Fell from Long Rigg Beck

CARLIN GILL & FELL HEAD

The hidden ravines of Carlin Gill make a fascinating objective preceding a contrastingly open fellwalk

START *Carlingill Bridge (SD 624995; CA10 3XX)*

DISTANCE *5¼ miles (8½km)*

ORDNANCE SURVEY 1:25,000 MAP
Explorer OL19 - Howgill Fells/Upper Eden Valley

ACCESS *Start from a small roadside parking area on Fairmile Road just south of the bridge. Not for the genteel, the ravine could also be dangerous if wet or wintry. •OPEN ACCESS - see page 8.*

From the single-arched bridge turn to follow Carlingill Beck upstream, with a rough little path materialising. An early impasse forces you higher, meeting a better path that slants back down to the bank just beyond a colourful confluence with Weasel Gill. This lengthy approach to the ravines is largely a delight, and even when the path is less clear, the route is not in question. The slopes increasingly close in, and at the second inflowing stream on the right (Small Gill), the valley narrows markedly: you might cross to an easier strath a little before this lovely confluence which merits a break before things gets more dramatic.

If not already there, now cross to the opposite bank of the now deeply carved gill, where a clear little path rises above a rocky impasse and on through a small patch of scree. This cautious but delectable traverse quickly leads to the foot of the ravine of Black Force on the opposite bank. *This is a series of tumbling little falls throughout the full length of a dark-walled gorge.* Keeping faith with the floor of Carlin Gill, a small path remains on this north side for a while, then at a rocky impasse it crosses the stream and the way forges spiritedly on through the bouldery environs of the narrow floor. The gill soon bends right to pass a lovely waterslide, and this absorbing path is soon halted at the emphatic impasse of The Spout, depositing you neatly on a perfect viewing platform. *This stunning waterfall is not fully seen until penetrating to this very limit of exploration: well-named, it pours into a colourful amphitheatre.*

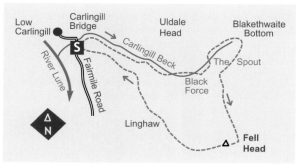

Escape by crossing the stream to a choice of a steep, grassy pull or a cleaner scramble up tilted rock: either demands caution, while the latter earns a more intimate view of The Spout. On the flank above you have a further choice, simplest being to turn right to trace the upper stream through its easing ravine. Alternatively, ascend steep grass for some time to meet a sheeptrod: turning right to contour along, it fades before you angle gently down to the reedy hollow of Blakethwaite Bottom. *After the claustrophobia of Carlin Gill, this basin is a contrastingly spacious upland.* However reaching it, cross the lesser, left-hand beck above the confluence, then on a little further to meet a path which doubles back right to ford the main arm of the beck (Great Ulgill Beck).

A little caution in route-finding is recommended here. Head directly away from the stream on a slender path rising slightly to a small patch of reeds. Beyond them, ignore a clearer little path heading off above but parallel with the gill, and instead make a steep little pull up the bank to the left. This rapidly eases to find a clearer trod commencing a gentle rise. Fell Head is up to the left, and Carlin Gill's depths are hidden down to the right. However, within 200 yards, and just as your way briefly levels in front of another reedy patch, opt for a thinner but clear trod slanting left up onto Ulgill Rigg. This climbs away to fade on reaching a broad, tilted shelf. Simply cross this slight rise to re-commence the ascent proper, with various trods and quad tracks playing a cat & mouse game as you scale the peaceful, easy slopes. *Look back to appraise the most tranquil of Howgills scenes, featuring a group of almost identical, unfrequented lesser tops.*

A better path might be found nearer the top to ease out and suddenly arrive on the well-defined summit ridge, with a big open view of The Calf group ahead. The summit cairn should also be seen, just a couple of minutes to the right along the broad ridge path. *At 2100ft/640m Fell Head is the third of the five Howgills' 2000-footers, lower than The Calf and Calders (WALK 20) but loftier than Yarlside and Randygill Top (WALK 24). Its 'outpost' situation makes it a superb all-round viewpoint, not only for its numerous Howgills' neighbours, but also looking down on the Lune Gorge, across to the Whinfell Ridge and the skyline of Lakeland.*

Depart by continuing along the ridge, through a minor dip and quickly up to a lesser cairn on the western top, another good place to linger. Descent proper begins directly from it on an initially thin trod dropping north-west, bound for the distinct knoll of Linghaw some distance below. A delectable path winds invitingly down Blake Ridge, Fell Head's north-western spur. Soon becoming a clearer quad track, keep left at an early fork to drop unfailingly down to a saddle featuring a crossroads of green ways in front of Linghaw. Keep straight on the broad quad track making the short pull to its unmarked grassy brow at 1640ft/500m.

Remain on this broad track maintaining the north-westerly downhill direction. With the Lune Gorge outspread below, the finish is an obvious one, this infallible track tracing the long spine of the fell high above the Carlin Gill edge. *For a while there is a good prospect up the ravine to The Spout.* Only on the lower slopes does this super track falter: as a tractor track takes over keep to the Carlin Gill edge, and though it tends to fade somewhat, easy terrain quickly leads back to the road.

Opposite: The Calf group from Fell Head

Carlingill Beck

FOX'S PULPIT

Firbank Fell offers glorious panoramas of the Howgills, while the return leg shadows the Lune along their base

START Lowgill (SD 620964; LA8 0BL)

DISTANCE 7 miles (11km)

ORDNANCE SURVEY 1:25,000 MAP
Explorer OL19 - Howgill Fells/Upper Eden Valley

ACCESS Start from Crook of Lune Bridge, down a side road from Lowgill's staggered crossroads. Small parking areas on either side. This corner is also known as Beck Foot.

Dating possibly from almost 500 years ago, beautiful Crook of Lune Bridge curves at each end then inclines to a narrow crest. From the bridge head west up the lane towards the viaduct, but quickly turn left over a bridge to pass between two fine houses, and a gate at the back sends a sunken way slanting up the field. *Good views look over the bridge to the western Howgill Fells.* At the top advance on to Davy Bank Farm at the end, just past which the very short drive runs out under a rail arch to join the B6257.

From the right-hand gate opposite ascend by a wall, soon using a gate to cross it and join a cart-track. This weaves uphill, doubling back and becoming grassier as it climbs. Meeting a fence ascend pleasantly with it, gaining the brow at a gate at a wall corner, with High House Farm down to the right. *The Lune Gorge is well seen to the right, while the Lakeland Fells appear ahead.* Through the gate you meet an enclosed cart-track rising from the farm: at this path crossroads, leave the bridleway and turn left up the pathless field, following the left-hand wall through further stiles, over a gentle brow and down to cross the tiny outflow of a small marsh. Here a stile conveys you to the other side of the wall to follow a sunken way up to a gate onto the Firbank Fell road.

Turn left, briefly uphill to gain the walk's highest point at some 997ft/304m on Hilltop Heights, all part of an undulating stride along its almost traffic-free course. *The western Howgills dominate this walk, most impressively so during this march along the fell road. Enjoy also views down the Lune Valley as far as the Bowland moors.* Before long the route rises again to gain Fox's Pulpit. *Firbank Fell is a place of pilgrimage by virtue of the windswept corner known as Fox's Pulpit. Here in 1652, and fresh from his vision on Pendle Hill, George Fox addressed a multitude that began the Quaker movement. Adjacent to a memorial tablet is a tiny graveyard.*

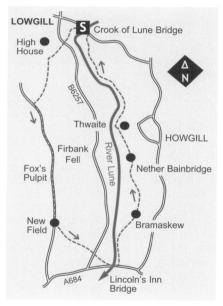

On resuming, the dead-straight road declines gradually to pass a lone house, and at the next cluster (New Field) turn left along a rough lane before the main buildings. Before its demise take a stile on the right, and slant across to a gate. Now slant down to the opposite far corner, and through the gate drop briefly right with the beginnings of a stream before crossing left on a low bank to an outer wall corner. Not quite as per map, here drop down a short row of trees to a stile into Hawkrigg Wood, through which a lovely path slants down. Emerging at a stile, maintain the slant left to an old hedge corner, below which is a gate onto the B6257. A few strides right is a ladder-stile sending you to a like stile, then over a low brow to drop steeply to a stile alongside the farm at Lincoln's Inn Bridge. *Note the super barn attached to this former hostelry.*

Across the bridge, a gate on the left begins the long return up the Lune. As the remainder of the walk follows the Dales Way, all its waymarks are relevant. Heading along the charming riverbank the Lune Viaduct soon appears, with a footbridge on Crosdale Beck accessing it. *Red sandstone and metal arches loom dramatically above a pastoral scene, a relic of the Clapham-Lowgill branch.* The way passes under the tall arches before slanting uphill. On fading, ascend a little further and cross to a corner stile/gate opposite, from where a fieldside track heads away with the parallel beck to Low Branthwaite. Cross the farm drive to a stile opposite, then rise across the field to an old wall corner. A path materialises to rise left, becoming briefly enclosed. On emerging ignore the drive to Bramaskew Farm, ahead, and take a stile to its left. *Firbank church is seen across the valley, above the grassy line of the old railway.*

Continue past the farm to a stile at the end, and continue away down a large field to pass a small barn in a hollow. Keeping left of a wall beyond, a cart track becomes enclosed to lead to Nether Bainbridge. Without entering its confines take a stile on the left, tracing the wall up to the field corner: ignoring a stile here go left with the facing wall. Use a gate further along to rise to a little brow, then descend to Hole House Farm. Entering its yard, bear left between dwellings to a gate. A footbridge crosses Smithy Beck and a path drops left to a stile. Now cross to accompany the Lune through a large pasture below Thwaite Farm.

Here you encounter the river at close quarters, its stony bank leading the eye to Fell Head, westernmost 2000-footer of the Howgills. This final stage is a lovely ramble, the intermittently wooded bank rich in springtime flowers. A footbridge crosses Chapel Beck and the river remains close all the way to a point at the end of a slim enclosure where, ignoring a fence ahead with a fishing hut in the field beyond, the path instead bears right to a gate below Crook of Lune Farm. Advance a little further to meet a grassy way, which is followed left to join a narrow road down to Crook of Lune Bridge.

GREEN BELL

*Rolling hills, outstanding views and near-perfect
solitude high above a lovely old village*

START *Ravenstonedale (NY 723042; CA17 4NG)*

DISTANCE *6^{1}4 miles (10km)*

ORDNANCE SURVEY 1:25,000 MAP
Explorer OL19 - Howgill Fells/Upper Eden Valley

ACCESS *Start from the village centre. Roadside parking.
Infrequent Sedbergh-Kirkby Stephen bus.*
•OPEN ACCESS - see page 8.

Ravenstonedale is one of the prettiest of old Westmorland
villages, nestling at the foot of the Howgill Fells but also set below
a limestone landscape spread to the north. A homely cluster of
dwellings sit respectfully back from the attractive church. St
Oswald's dates from the mid-18th century, and overlooks the site
of a 12th century cell of Gilbertine canons. The King's Head and
the Black Swan with a shop sit amid pleasant beck scenery - look
out for a surviving spinning gallery within the delights of this old
village known locally as 'Rassendl'.

From the junction outside the school turn through the churchyard, passing left of the church to a gate out of the far end. Across
sports fields drop down between buildings to emerge alongside the
King's Head. Turn left on the through road here, soon leaving the

village. Before reaching the by-pass, turn left up a 'no through road' to Greenside. It is left at the first gate on the right, following the wall away through a couple of fields to enter an enclosed green lane. *Green Bell forms a large dome up to the left. These modest pastures mark the important Lune/Eden watershed, the major North-South Cumbrian divide with one river bound for Carlisle, the other for Lancaster.* When it prematurely expires maintain the same line, and at the field-end transfer to the other side of the wall. Emerging from brief enclosure, leave the wall and slant left down across the field to a bridle-gate in the opposite wall. An old way drops down past a barn and out over a small bridge to reach a drive onto an access road at The Hollow.

Go left on the road up towards a brow, and as the adjacent wall turns sharp right, instead turn sharp left onto the open moor, using the left-hand of two tractor tracks heading away onto the broad northern flanks of Green Bell. From gaining the open moor here, the initially poor route to the summit is already largely obvious. Ignoring the moisture of Tailor Mire to the right, the track makes a cautious start on the slope ahead. Occasionally sketchy,

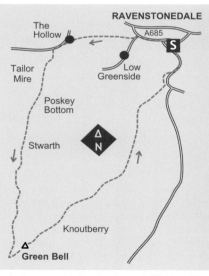

it rises to a brief leveling at the marshy beginnings of Wythe Mire dropping left. Continuing, the initially firm track soon downgrades to a simple trod, which begins a more earnest ascent through far nicer terrain. This grand section rises to merge into a grassy patch that has long been visible. Ascend this, and a thin trod rises to the skyline just above to put you onto the end of the knoll of Stwarth.

The summit re-appears ahead, as well as the minor edge of Hunthoof Pike in front. Keep to the right along this marshy shelf, a path re-forming at the end to recommence ascent. As an old sunken way curves left, you merge into a broader track from the right. The true ascent resumes, slanting left up past unseen Hunthoof Pike. The old way comes up from the left to cross your route, and while you could simply continue up your direct way to the summit, it is far better to veer right on the old way, slanting mercurially across Green Bell's upper cone. *As great views look down over Great Swindale to the right, a true sense of really being on the fells prevails.*

At the end you arrive on a saddle to the south-west of the top, a supreme moment looking ahead to Yarlside. From here a clear path doubles back left up to the waiting Ordnance column at 1985ft/605m. *Green Bell is arguably the finest sub-2000ft viewpoint for the varied mountain groups of England. Distantly is the serrated skyline of Lakeland, a joy to find in any picture; to the north the less dramatic but nonetheless powerful Cross Fell range; from east to south are the individual summits of the Dales; while in front are the Howgills themselves, appearing in style as a well-defined mountain group. This is a grand place to be.*

The summit is vacated by a thin path heading north-east (not a thinner one further right, bound for Grere Fell), almost at once dropping steeply to the low but substantial remains of a sheepfold. *The springs of Dale Gill below the fold are generally regarded as being the true source of the River Lune.* Ravenstonedale is already in view, and the finest way back takes the thin trod through a minor saddle and up to the cairned minor top of Knoutberry. Continue north-east utilising occasional trods where possible, down along the broad crest of Snowfell End from where resume, aiming for the far end of a large island field visible ahead. At the bottom a path is picked up to drop down to cross meandering Wyegarth Gill.

Ascending the bank a path runs to a minor brow and then down to pick up a good green track descending the fell. This narrows between enclosing walls, becoming a firmer track beyond a bottle-neck mire and keeping with the right-hand wall to reach a gate off the fell alongside Kilnmire. Continue along the access road to the village edge at Town Head. An interesting finish delays the tarmac by crossing to between a brace of wooden bridges on the left, thence dropping down through the 'back' of the village.

YARLSIDE RIDGE

A steep climb to shapely heights with outstanding views

START *Cautley (SD 698969; LA10 5LY)*

DISTANCE *6 miles (9^{1}2km)*

ORDNANCE SURVEY 1:25,000 MAP
Explorer OL19 - Howgill Fells/Upper Eden Valley

ACCESS *Start from the Cross Keys Inn on the A683. Lay-by just past it. Infrequent Sedbergh-Kirkby Stephen bus.*
•OPEN ACCESS - see page 8.

For a note on Cautley, see page 92. From the parking area drop down to a footbridge over the Rawthey. *Pause already to appraise Great Dummacks downstream: this is the fell that boasts Cautley Crag as its own.* Across, a good path heads away downstream above the Rawthey, quickly swinging in to the prized amphitheatre beneath Cautley Crag. Passing above a footbridge on adjacent Cautley Holme Beck, the path is infallibly drawn towards the base of the falls, surmounting a gentle spur that undulates along to the foot of the ravine. Here the path forks: leaving the left branch for WALK 25, take the contrastingly genteel right branch rising through bracken. Without the rigours of the other path, this still affords a classic prospect of the tumbling falls of the Spout. The path slants up above the sidestream as a delectable green way, zigzagging and becoming a little stony part way up to arrive on the saddle of Bowderdale Head. *Beyond, the long valley of Bowderdale runs northwards towards the upper Lune Valley.*

Advance along the near side of this marshy saddle until just short of the negligible highest point, where the second half of your ascent begins. A thin but clear trod breaks off to slant up to the right, and across to approach a grassy ravine between yourself and Yarlside's main bulk. Deflected more directly uphill above it, the trod turns to run in towards its upper reach, then

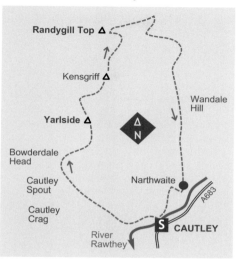

fades. Now simply turn more directly uphill on steep grassy slopes to your right to gain the skyline, and advance just a few strides further to meet a path in the saddle between Yarlside's rounded south top (right) and its summit (left). Go left on this grand little path which enjoys a short pull onto Yarlside's summit, marked by a lonely cairn at 2096ft/639m. *This otherwise bare top is a fine, airy vantage point. Look back to see the upper section of Cautley Spout, with Great Dummacks, Calders, Bram Rigg Top and The Calf behind, and the northern Howgills ridges arrayed. Eastwards are the Howgills' neighbours Wild Boar, Swarth and Baugh Fells.*

Resume north-west on a thin path along the ridge, avoiding thoughts of a bee-line for Kensgriff. *You are now amid a real Howgills atmosphere, with ridges and tops outspread, and looking directly down Bowderdale at this point. Shapely Kensgriff, next along the ridge, is currently dwarfed by your present fell, but not so in 10 minutes time when looking up to it!* A trod from the cairn peters out on the steep northerly edge (in mist you could continue too far down), and steep grassy slopes angle you right, down to the col, with Kensgriff looking a fine little cone. Across a few marshy strides a thin path makes a direct ascent of its ridge. Ignoring an early thinner quad bike track slanting left, you will quickly gain the small, lonely cairn at 1883ft/574m. *Looking back, it will be seen why the direct approach was not recommended, Yarlside's scree slope being far too rough for comfort.*

Resume north again, with another modest path descending the easy-angled ridge to a saddle containing a pool beneath Randygill Top's dull slope. Ahead, Green Bell is also prominent. To claim your second 2000-footer, remain on the path aiming for the left side of the col in front of Randygill Top, a good straight path dropping directly to marginally below the actual saddle, crossing its left side to then ascend the grassy slopes. Your trod ends at a cross-path, though a faint quad track just to the left possibly helps a little. Towards the top this fades, and here bear left on easy ground to gain the summit ridge, with the cairn a little further left. *Yet again, a solid cairn sits in loneliness. At 2047ft/624m this is the lowest of the five 2000ft mountains within the Howgills, but its panorama is as good as any, from the Lakeland Fells to the North Pennines, and all around the northern Dales.*

Leave the cairn by heading north-east on the right-hand of two departing paths across the tiny summit pool, declining gently towards the prominent Green Bell. This grand high-level traverse on a sumptuous green pathway drops steadily to the well-defined saddle under Stockless. At this very point drop right a few feet only to pick up the beginnings of a trod shown on the map as a public footpath. Turn right on this to run a splendid course across the upper flanks of Randygill Top, contouring along high above the beginnings of Stockless Gill. It then drops a little to the head of a grassy ravine, then opening out more on easier slopes. Here leave the contouring path and slant left down to the base of a large reedy patch at the head of the gill. Across, pick up an old part-sunken path to lead down above the gill. When it fades simply forge on down the slope, well above the stream until aiming for a distinct confluence with Spen Gill beneath a rocky ravine ahead. *This is a fine spot to linger awhile and savour the charms as a couple of tasty waterfalls tumble through the rocky surrounds.*

From the confluence either climb directly up to quickly reach a reedy track, or first go left up the bank to see more of the ravine before crossing reedy ground to find an initially faint old track on Wandale Hill's flank. Either way, turn right along this old trackway, soon leaving the marshy section behind for a contrastingly splendid green march. *To the right Yarlside and Kensgriff are well displayed.*

Simply remain on this track, becoming firmer as it joins a wall and runs above the old farmhouse of Mountain View. *This derelict farmstead boasts one of the finest locations in the district.* The way continues, keeping right at a fork to angle down to a gate. In similar fashion it runs down the wallside to become an old sunken lane above the farm of Narthwaite. Entering the yard, turn right between barns to a gate down to the right into a grassy enclosure. A path winds down to the bottom right corner, where an enclosed way runs down to a ford on Backside Beck. Reasonable stepping-stones make for an easy crossing in normal conditions, though in spate, wet feet would be easily acquired. *In extremis, return to Narthwaite and down its drive to the road at Handley's Bridge.* With the end just minutes away now, the path runs left up outside the trees and delightfully on through open country, back on Yarlside's base to drop gently back to your opening steps by the footbridge on the Rawthey.

Kensgriff from under Randygill Top

CAUTLEY SPOUT & CRAG

A famous corner of the Howgills, the splendour of Cautley Spout leading to an airy felltop and a gentle descent

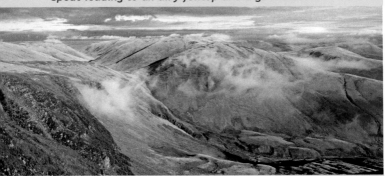

START *Cautley (SD 698969; LA10 5LY)*

DISTANCE *5^{1}2 miles (9km)*

ORDNANCE SURVEY 1:25,000 MAP
Explorer OL19 - Howgill Fells/Upper Eden Valley

ACCESS *Start from the Cross Keys Inn on the A683.
Lay-by just past it. Infrequent Sedbergh-Kirkby Stephen bus.*
•OPEN ACCESS - see page 8.

Cautley Crag and Spout combine to form the grandest scene in the Howgill Fells. The steep crag extends for the best part of a mile to an abrupt end at the Spout. Cautley Spout is a series of waterfalls which tumble in rapid succession for several hundred feet to the valley floor. Boasting one of the finest settings in the Dales, the Cross Keys is that rare creature the temperance inn: offering welcome refreshments, its legacy ensures it is never likely to offer a pint of ale. It bears a 1732 datestone. Though labelled Cautley there is no definable centre, just a scattering of farms, dwellings, a church and a Methodist Chapel on the Sedbergh road.

From the parking area drop down to a footbridge over the Rawthey. *Already you will pause here to appraise Great Dummacks downstream: this is the fell that boasts Cautley Crag as its own.* Across, a good path heads away downstream above the Rawthey, quickly swinging in to the prized amphitheatre beneath Cautley Crag. Passing above a footbridge on adjacent Cautley Holme Beck, the path is infallibly drawn towards the base of the falls, surmounting a gentle spur that undulates along to the foot of the ravine. Here the path forks, with the right branch climbing to Bowderdale Head. Your left branch crosses a tiny sidestream to tackle the steep climb by the gill. Very quickly you reach the start of a stone path, superbly engineered to make life easier in addition to its principal purpose of helping to prevent erosion. It winds ever cleverly up above the ravine: extra caution is urged when peering into the lower fall, which is partly obscured by hardy foliage. *Pausing to look back, Wild Boar Fell, Swarth Fell and Baugh Fell together form a sombre mountain skyline.*

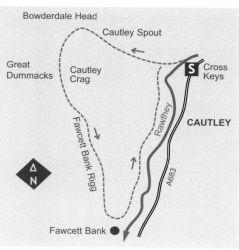

Further up, the upper falls are free of obstruction and can be savoured more leisurely. Virtually at the top of these the steepest section ends at a small platform: the much gentler continuation left begins with a tiny rock band, then runs splendidly on, looking straight towards the uppermost falls. Crossing the sidestream of Swere Gill, it rises round to meet the main stream at the very top of the falls, Red Gill Beck. Though the main path continues upstream, cross here and locate a faint trod onto the spur of Great Dummacks above Cautley Crag. This same path broadens and leads increasingly gently up the broadening spur above Cautley Crag, all the way to the highest point. The upper stages run along the grassy crest of the crags to reveal some dramatic moments. At the far end a stony gully is the place to break journey. *This provides a suitable foreground to the crag as it shrinks away towards the Spout: Yarlside forms an impressive wall behind, with Bowderdale running away beyond the dip of Bowderdale Head. The tame slopes of The Calf rise to the Howgills' plateau. Immediately above you is the summit of Great Dummacks, though few are likely to go seeking the errant high point of this broad plateau. At 2175ft/663m this is the least notable of the 2000ft tops of the Howgills - or at least it would be, if it wasn't for Cautley Crag....*

From your high point head south, bearing slightly away from the declining edge (aiming for distant Ingleborough, if clear), to

gain the more rounded end atop the broad ridge of Fawcett Bank Rigg. This makes for a super ramble after all the excitement of Cautley Spout. *Glorious views look out over several miles of the Rawthey's course to a mountain panorama, with Wild Boar Fell, Swarth Fell and Baugh Fell opposite, and the Dales' peaks dominated as ever by the celebrated Three Peaks triumvirate of Penyghent, Ingleborough and Whernside.*

Cautley Spout

*Opposite:
Great Dummacks
and Cautley Crag
from the Rawthey*

Simply stride down this gentle ridge, a splendid quad bike track soon forming, until approaching a wall corner near the base of the ridge. Here deflect left with the wall, and at the next corner drop steeply down by it to gain the Sedbergh-Cautley bridle-way. Turn left on this path and it will lead unfailingly back, the Rawthey Valley making fine company from your terrace well above the river. *Besides the fells opposite, you have the easternmost Howgills pairing of Wandale Hill and Harter Fell ahead. St Mark's church stands on the roadside below.*

After a spell along the base of the fell, the path escapes the bracken at a bridle-gate into rough pasture. Beyond a second gate the path is fainter until resurrected at a stream ahead. On again, and beyond a gateway in an old wall, a gate on the left returns the path through the intake wall to the base of the fell. Resume as before, soon dropping to take the right-hand of adjacent gates where a briefly enclosed section leads to Cautley Holme Beck, just short of its confluence with the Rawthey. A footbridge upstream leads back into the basin of Cautley Crag, with the outgoing path just a few strides ahead to finish as you began.

INDEX • *Walk number refers*